THE 90-DAY MORNING DEVOTIONAL

THE
90-DAY
MORNING DEVOTIONAL

Inspiring Devotions to Start Your Day with God

Karianna Frey, MS

ROCKRIDGE
PRESS

To the one holding this book, you are fearfully and wonderfully made.

Interior and Cover Designer: Scott Wooledge
Art Producer: Tom Hood
Editor: Chloe Moffett
Production Editor: Holland Baker
Production Manager: Eric Pier-Hocking

Author photo courtesy of Tina Pham

Paperback ISBN: 978-1-63807-210-2
eBook ISBN: 978-1-63807-592-9
R0

Ad
majorem Dei
gloriam!

Introduction

According to a 2009 study published in the *European Journal of Social Psychology*, it takes around 66 days to start a habit, be it good or bad. I am great at starting new habits and terrible at maintaining them, unless there is a challenge involved, especially one with a finite end. Whether we are talking about a "Mile a Day in May," "Planksgiving," or "Frocktober," the idea of challenging myself to something new not only taps into my competitive side but also helps me discover something new about myself. Plus, by the time I get to the end of the challenge, I've usually developed a brand-new habit to celebrate!

My name is Karianna. I am a speaker, educator, author, wife, and mother. I have followed Christ since I was a young girl and I love making new-to-me discoveries in my Bible. The Bible is my anchor when I am feeling tossed on the waves, it is my rock when the ground is shifting beneath my feet, and it is my trusted counselor when I need a guiding hand.

Daily reading of the Bible is a fantastic habit to start! In your hands, you hold an invitation to join me and countless others on a 90-day journey that will take you on an exploration of the Bible and into a new routine with God at your side. For me, in my Christian identity, the Bible is not only a source of comfort and wisdom, but a way to have a dialogue with the creator of the universe whenever I need to. For the next 90 days, you will have a chance to meet God through a carefully curated selection of Bible verses and reflect on

what these eternal words mean to YOU. I will share a bit of commentary on God's love and discipline in my life as well as a bit of history. You will also meet some of my favorite thinkers and role models. The verses chosen are from the New King James Version (NKJV), with a few noted exceptions. Personally, I love the lyrical and poetic quality of this translation; however, you are more than welcome to use this devotional alongside your own Bible (either in hard copy, online, or on your mobile device) to read the verses in full context.

The Bible is a living library that has persisted through the ages for good reason. The Bible does not care if you are Catholic or Protestant; it is there for each of us, as long as we are willing to be open to what God has in store for us. Every time you experience a new book, chapter, or verse of the Bible, you will make a new discovery about God, the world around you, or even yourself. You will not find dogma or theological arguments in these pages, but rather an invitation to spend a few minutes of each of the next 90 days basking in the love of the One who fearfully and wonderfully made you (Psalm 139).

I'm excited to have you join me on this journey. Let's dive in.

How to Use This Devotional

Starting a new routine takes patience and grace. Take as much time as you need to sit with each prompt. It may take you more than a day to really dig into the guiding questions and actions, and that's okay. Let the Holy Spirit guide your steps and your time as you use the verses, reflections, questions, actions, and guided prayer to wade even deeper into the living water of Christ. Our goal over the next 90 days is not perfection but progress. Each of us will have a different way to embark on this journey and different times that work for us to meet God during the day.

For some, diving into this devotional first thing in the morning will be the best way to spend time with God, cozying up in a favorite reading spot with a blanket and a cuppa, and basking in the glory of God's creation as the sun rises over the horizon.

Some of you will meet God during your midday break to pause and take a breath after the morning's activities, conversing with God over lunch or a snack and getting energized for what the rest of the day has ready for you.

And some of you will find it works best to meet God in the evening, thanking Him for the blessings bestowed on you throughout the day, and stilling your heart and listening as the chirping crickets and croaking frogs lull you into a bit of quietude for the evening.

Each day will include a Bible verse, my commentary, and then three opportunities for you to engage more deeply with the scripture. With Jesus as your living water, you will be invited to "wade in the water" by pondering thought-provoking questions, taking a daily action step to tie everything together, and finishing in prayer.

During this journey, you will be invited to deepen your communication and share your heart with God in the form of journaling, and I encourage you to keep a separate journal nearby. Make this devotional your own by underlining, highlighting, using sticky notes, or dog-earing pages that you want to come back to time and again. Break the binding, spill coffee on it, let your tears leave their trace. Start on Day 1 or Day 90, or open up to a random day and see what is waiting for you. If you miss a day, don't fret; just pick up where you left off. You might even use it only on the weekends, and that's okay. This time is for just you and God.

Our God is not a demanding God. He does not ask that we set an appointment to meet with Him, nor will He shame us if we don't speak to Him for some time. We are His beloved creation, and He is a loving Father, waiting for us with open arms.

This is the day that the Lord has made; let us rejoice and be glad in it.

—Psalm 118:24 (NRSV)

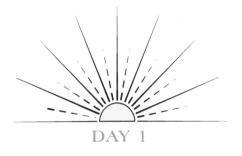

An Oasis in the Desert

The Lord will guide you continually,
and satisfy your soul in drought, and strengthen your
bones; you shall be like a watered garden, and like
a spring of water, whose waters do not fail.

—Isaiah 58:11

I am a terrible plant mom. I have friends who can just look at a plant and have it become lush and green and full of life. I can't even keep a cactus from dying. But I think I have it figured out . . . it's the water. I just can't seem to get the watering right. Either I'm watering too much or I'm watering too little; either way, without the right amount of water, my plants are not going to live long.

There is a good reason water is mentioned throughout the Bible. The Israelites and first-century Christians lived in dry, arid regions, and the importance of water was well known. Without water, crops can't grow. Without water, animals die. Without water, we die. The Bible says Jesus is our living water, giving us eternal life. God's Word is described as water, bringing relief to our dry spiritual lives. In Isaiah 58, God promises His people that they will become like a watered garden that never runs dry. God never breaks his promises to us; however, we are challenged to change our ways. We are called to live a life of sacrifice, service, and satisfaction in God alone. Sacrifice, service, satisfaction: none of these are easy to do on our own, and luckily we do not have to. Not only do we have others to walk this path with us, but we have Jesus to guide us.

We can all be well-watered people. We can choose to spend time in God's Word on a daily basis. We can let our water overflow to those around us. We can allow our actions to produce fruit in ourselves and others. We can be an oasis in the desert (even if we kill cacti).

Wade in the Water

- How does starting your day with Jesus influence the rest of your day?

- What areas in your life are most in need of life-giving water?

Daily Action

Drink your water today! Aim for 64 fluid ounces (1.9 liters) today and see how your body responds. Drink your first glass with your Bible next to you as you read through all of Isaiah 58.

Guided Prayer

Dearest Jesus, there is nothing this world can offer to me that is better than You. Thank You for watering me and helping me bloom. Amen.

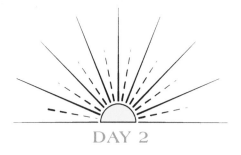

Simple Gifts

As each one has received a gift, minister it to one another, as good stewards of the manifold grace of God.

—*1 Peter 4:10*

Our God is a loving Father, and like most loving fathers, He delights in giving gifts to His children. We are not talking about fancy cars or houses, but rather the gifts that make each and every one of us unique creations. The gifts that have been given to us by God are not just for us alone; rather, God expects us to be good stewards of our gifts and to use them to minister to, help, and support one another.

There is one caveat, however, and that is that not all of us are given the same gifts. What delight would there be if we were all excellent speakers, or could all write a bestselling novel, or could take home Olympic medals? What would the benefit be if we were all the same? God loves diversity, and that includes diversity among our gifts. It can be easy to get caught up in comparing our gifts to the gifts of others, telling ourselves that our gifts are not good enough, or that our gifts are worthless because in our minds they are not important. This is when the trouble comes, because competition is an easy way to sow division and discord, especially in the body of Christ.

No matter what gifts God has given to you, know that they are important and they serve a specific purpose. We are all called to use our gifts for the glory of God. It is when we use our gifts for this purpose that they have their highest value and potential. So, whether your gift is that of song, speech, hospitality, kindness, generosity, or athletic prowess, do it "ad majorem Dei gloriam," for the greater glory of God.

Wade in the Water

- Do you see your gifts as having less value than others? What can you do to better value the gifts God gave you?

- How can you better use your gifts to glorify God? Are there opportunities in your community or home where your talents can be of use?

Daily Action

In your journal, make a list of your spiritual gifts. Let your imagination run and do not hold yourself back! Next to each gift, note how you can best use it to glorify God.

Guided Prayer

Dear God, You are the giver of all good things. Help me not only see my gifts but to use them for Your glory. Amen.

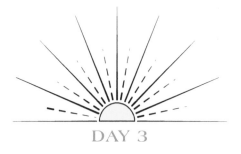

Today Is an Opportunity for Good

*Therefore, as we have opportunity, let us do good to all,
especially to those who are of the household of faith.*

—Galatians 6:10

What does it mean to have an opportunity? We hear in passing talk about the "opportunity of a lifetime" or "opportunities that we can't refuse," but what exactly is the apostle Paul speaking about when he writes to the church at Galatia about having opportunity? We are given the opportunity, in our time on earth, to affect the world around us, both for good and for bad. What would it look like if we not only had the time to do good for all people, but chose to use that time to do good for all people, especially those in the family of believers? What would it look like to truly walk in the Spirit and bear one another's burdens as a family?

Our actions (what we do) are what give us the right to be listened to by others. For the family of believers, the saying "actions speak louder than words" becomes even more apparent. If your daily actions do not match the words that come out of your mouth, your words are as useless as a screen door on a submarine. Every morning, we wake up to another opportunity to honor God with our words and actions. Do we take it?

It is easy for us to have pride when we think what we are doing is right and to look down on those we think are doing wrong, judging them for their fall. However, we should also acknowledge and remember how easy it is to fall out of our relationship with Christ, because we are human and we all fall short of the grace of God. When that happens, we too need the support of others to help us restore that relationship. Families help one another; not just when it is convenient, but always.

Wade in the Water

- How can you treat all Christians as members of your family, not allowing for denominational differences?

- How inviting are your actions to others outside of your faith tradition? In what ways do you share Christ's love with others without saying a word?

Daily Action

Keep yourself open to the opportunities that God places in your path today. Is there a tear you can dry? A burden you can bear? Maybe it's the chance to feed a stranger's parking meter or to share a smile with someone you pass on the street. How will you interact with others today?

Guided Prayer

Lord, give me the opportunity to truly honor You through my actions with my fellow family members. Amen.

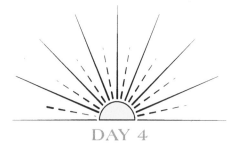

Working for Others Instead of Ourselves

For we are His workmanship, created in Christ Jesus for good works, which God prepared beforehand that we should walk in them.

—*Ephesians 2:10*

The question "Why did God make me?" is not just for brooding philosophy students or curious kindergarteners; this is a question that all of us face at some point in our lives. For what purpose did God choose to create humanity? Depending on your faith tradition, there are a few different answers to this question. But Paul, in his letter to the Ephesians, does a great job of explaining it: We were created by God to do His good works.

Notice I did not say we were created by God to do our good works; I can say for certain that what I want to do and what God wants me to do don't always match up. On chilly mornings, I want to stay warm and snuggly in my bed, but God wants me to joyfully get up and help lead my family into the day, setting an example by serving others before serving myself. So, I get up, not just with my own strength, but through the strength of Christ dwelling within me. The same strength that Christ used to bear His cross is the strength that I use to die to self and serve others joyfully.

It is through Christ dwelling in us that we are called to—and are able to—continue the works that He started so long ago. It is through Christ that I am called to share the Gospel. It is through Christ that I am called to encourage others into a relationship with Him. It is through Christ that I am able to reach out to those that society has cast aside. It is through Christ that I can do all things, not because of who I am, but because of He who is in me.

Wade in the Water

- How can you more joyfully accept the work God puts before you?

- In what ways are your daily tasks part of the good works that God calls you to do?

Daily Action

Before beginning your day, make a list of the tasks and goals you would like to accomplish and the steps you'll take to get there. Take a moment to pray for God's blessing on your tasks and goals (no matter how mundane!) and that God's will is done through you.

Guided Prayer

Help me be aware that I do all things through Christ in me, and may I never take for granted any of the good works that You have prepared for me, Father. Amen.

Saved through Mercy

*But when the kindness and the love of God
our Savior toward man appeared, not by works of
righteousness which we have done, but according
to His mercy He saved us, through the washing
of regeneration and renewing of the Holy Spirit.*

—*Titus 3:4–5*

When I was younger, I would spend many Saturday nights with my aunts who were so influential in my faith formation. Sunday mornings were filled with the soul-shaking strains of gospel music, and my aunt's absolute favorite was "Amazing Grace." For her, this simple hymn was an easy way to describe our walk with Christ and a beautiful reminder of something we can very easily forget—that we were *all lost* before Christ found us.

We live in a fallen world that is separated from its Creator. It is not always easy to live with or even be around others who do not know Christ. We can often find ourselves becoming more and more weary of having to justify our relationship with Christ. We may even have our faith mocked by those who don't understand or share it. The simple act of blessing our food in public may open us up to questions or even judgment. But we were all once slaves to our own desires, and God rescued us from ourselves. None of us are saved by our own actions. We are saved through the mercy of God and through His kindness and love for us. When we find ourselves frustrated with the world, let us remember that we are no different from that world except that we have accepted the mercy of God. It is through His mercy and grace that we have been found. If not for the grace of God, all of us would still be lost.

Wade in the Water

- Your salvation is freely given to you. Can you accept this as true?

- How can you follow Jesus's example of mercy when dealing with others?

Daily Action

Remember that you are a new creation because of God's mercy and grace. Take out your journal and reflect upon what it means to never need to *do* anything to earn salvation. How would your life be different if not for Christ's sacrifice?

Guided Prayer

Lord Jesus, when I am frustrated with the world around me, help me remember that it is through your grace that I have eternal life and that my life should be an invitation for others to follow you as well. Amen.

Faith and Action

A new commandment I give to you, that you love one another; as I have loved you, that you also love one another. By this all will know that you are My disciples, if you have love for one another.

—*John 13:34–45*

On the surface, Jesus's commandment to love one another seems very simple. But like most simple things, when you really get to the heart of it, there is nothing simple about it. It's easy to say that we love people, but it's much harder to *actually* love them.

Take a moment and think back to the last time someone really got on your nerves. Maybe it was the guy on the airplane who reclined his seat in front of you, causing your drink to suddenly lurch into your lap. Maybe it was the lady in line in front of you having the conversation on speakerphone. Maybe it was the driver who drove right through the stop sign when it was clearly your turn to go, or the brother-in-law who made fun of the gray in your hair. Maybe it's that coworker who, no matter what, just seems not to like you. In those moments, it may feel impossible to truly love those people, and yet that is what Jesus wants us to do. Truly loving someone is more than a feeling. It means seeing that person as Christ sees them and letting our actions reflect Christ's dwelling within us.

Jesus does not set up impossible tasks because He revels in watching us falter and fall. He gives us this commandment because as His disciples we are His students—and He is teaching us that with His help we are capable of so much more than we think. Great teachers do not let their students quit when the lesson gets hard; rather, they encourage them and challenge them to keep moving toward mastery. As Christians, one of our main lessons is learning to love one another, faults and all. It's a lesson that may take a lifetime, and that's okay.

Wade in the Water

- What habits or personality quirks do you find unlovable?

- Is it possible to love someone without really liking them? Why or why not?

Daily Action

Next time you are feeling the waves of irritation build inside of you because of another person, take a deep breath in, hold it for a count of four, and breathe it out. While you breathe, thank God for the chance to practice patience.

Guided Prayer

Father God, the world you created is a space for constant learning and exploring. Thank you for always teaching us through the gift of one another. Amen.

A Cry in the Night

*Therefore Eli said to Samuel, ". . . and it shall be, if
He calls you, that you must say, 'Speak, Lord, for Your
servant hears.'" . . . Now the Lord came and stood and
called as at other times, "Samuel! Samuel!" and Samuel
answered, "Speak, for Your servant hears."*

—1 Samuel 3:9–10

I n 1 Samuel, Eli is a man who is given a rare second chance to
make things right. As a high priest, Eli has a great many duties
at the temple, and as a father, he has two sons to raise. One
of these things he does better than the other. Eli's sons grow
to be less than virtuous men, and everyone around them knows it.
Eli bears the burden of not having parented his sons very well and
raising men who are not worthy of the blessing of God. Then along
comes Samuel.

Samuel is sent to Eli at a young age to learn from the aged
priest. One night, Samuel hears a voice calling him. Thinking that
the voice must be Eli, he runs to him. Eventually, Eli recognizes
that it is the voice of God calling to Samuel, something that his
own sons have never heard. Eli encourages Samuel to not only
listen but to respond.

There are times in our lives when we are Samuel, and there are times when we are Eli. Sometimes we need someone to show us where God's voice is coming from, and sometimes we need to encourage another person to say, "Speak, Lord, for your servant hears."

Our God loves second chances. No one is ever too far gone to restore their relationship with Him, not even Eli's sons. However, a relationship is a two-way street. Eli sees his chance for reconciliation—offering better guidance this time around—and takes it; Eli's sons don't.

Wade in the Water

- Why do we sometimes find it difficult to hear God's voice in our daily lives?

- Think of when you last replied to God with "Send me!" What was the outcome?

Daily Action

Next time you find yourself in a conversation, make a point of really focusing on the conversation at hand. Put your devices away, lay down your book or magazine, and give the other person your full attention so that you can listen, hear, and guide.

Guided Prayer

Dearest Lord, I don't always know when You are speaking to me. Please send others into my life to help my ears and heart to always be open to your voice. Amen.

Being Welcoming

[Be] rejoicing in hope, patient in tribulation,
continuing steadfastly in prayer; distributing to the
needs of the saints, given to hospitality.

—*Romans 12:12–13*

Hospitality is a big deal in the Bible. In the Old Testament, it is more than just a good deed; it is part of the written law. When you think about it, the area around Jerusalem was not the gentlest place. The environment is arid and rocky, and water was pretty hard to come by. The sun beats down relentlessly, and natural shelter was scarce. In short, a traveler would rely on the hospitality of those around them for his very survival.

Hospitality is modeled by Abraham when he invites three strangers (who turn out to be God's messengers in disguise) into his tent for food and water. Later, Rebecca's suitability as a wife for Isaac is confirmed by her act of taking care of a stranger's horses. And the New Testament missionaries are taught to use hospitality as an initial test to see whether a household or village will be receptive to hearing the Good News. If the household does not extend hospitality to the missionaries, they are to move on and not look back.

Hospitality has the power to cultivate connection, repair broken relationships, and strengthen existing ones—all it takes is an open hand and heart. We are all capable of hospitality and, no, it does not have to be picture-perfect. True hospitality is not about the perfect visual; it's about genuine love and concern for the comfort of another pilgrim on the journey.

Wade in the Water

- Why do you think the early missionaries relied on hospitality as a test for a new city?

- How do you show hospitality to those around you?

Daily Action

For many of us, hospitality is rooted in sharing meals. Begin to collect simple recipes that you can take to those in need or share with those around you. Make one today and share it with someone in need.

Guided Prayer

Hospitable God, caring for one another is not only good for the other person but also good for me. May my character, through Your indwelling, invite others to want to visit again. Amen.

A Relationship Built on Love

For God is not unjust to forget your work and labor of love which you have shown toward His name, in that you have ministered to the saints, and do minister.

—Hebrews 6:10

At its core, Christianity is a love story. It is about God, so in love with His creation that He is willing to give up everything to ensure that they stay with Him forever. I've had friends ask me why I believe in God, especially in light of so many injustices here on earth. Horrors like poverty, war, genocide, and hatred challenge the very idea of God's existence. They pose the classic question, "If God is so good, why is life so bad?"

For some, the answer is simple: This world is filled with terrible things and is not our final place; therefore, we should want to be somewhere other than here. We should align our thoughts and actions with the goal of getting away to heaven. Our time on earth is just a layover on the way to the eternal.

But for others, this world *is* filled with terrible things, and God has given us free will to help make it a little less terrible. We know God is real because we see the evidence of His heart in the charitable actions of those around us. We see God when we become His hands and feet, serving one another in love, not out of obligation. The Greek word *agape* is used to describe the love that God has for each of us and the love that we are called to have for one another. Agape is transcendent, universal, unconditional, and built on relationship—and it is through relationship that God is experienced.

Wade in the Water

- How can you better develop the desire to want to do work for others and not expect rewards or recognition?

- What are ways that you can serve others in secret?

Daily Action

When you give of your time, treasure, or talent, ask yourself whether you are giving out of obligation or out of love. In what ways can you make your giving less transactional and more of an act of worship— simple and humble?

Guided Prayer

Father God, it is so easy to give in to despair when faced with what is before us. Help me continue to fight the good fight until You call me home. Amen.

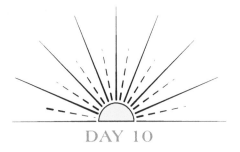

A People of Action

*Do you see that faith was working together with
His works, and by works faith was made perfect? ...
For as the body without the spirit is dead,
so faith without works is dead also.*

—James 2:22, 26

Which came first, the chicken or the egg? My son, a huge fan of chickens, loves to ponder this question. It's as old as time, a mystery of something that *is* versus something that *is to be*.

As followers of Christ, we have our own chicken-and-egg conundrum: Which is more important, faith or works? We don't just grapple with this in the 21st century; the church has pondered it for millennia. In his letter, James explains it pretty easily: Neither faith nor works is greater than the other and both are expected of the follower of Christ. While our salvation comes through our faith alone, we are created to do good works because that is what Christ did for us.

The entirety of Christ's ministry on earth was to set an example for all of us. Jesus did not just sit in the temple day in and day out, pondering the questions of the universe. He did not stay in His home, safe in the conviction that everything would be fine after His sacrifice and resurrection. He did not watch passively as people moved past him lost, broken, and seeking. No, Jesus went out among the people in the crowds, and ministered to them. He did not wait for them to come to Him; He went to them.

For many of us, our salvation, our adoption into the family of Christ, is only known by our good works. We as Christians are called to be known not only by our faith but also by our works.

Wade in the Water

- How does your faith influence how you love those around you? How does your love for Christ influence your actions toward others?

- Reflect on a time when you neglected to follow your faith with action or works. What happened? How could you have handled it differently?

Daily Action

Good works do not have to be big or grand. Sometimes the smallest action can make the biggest impact in someone's life. Make the decision to perform one small deed today.

Guided Prayer

Lord Jesus, thank you for your example of serving others. In a time when words can be meaningless, it is through our deeds that our identity in you becomes known to others. Amen.

You Don't Have to Be Alone

Though one may be overpowered by another, two can withstand him. And a threefold cord is not quickly broken.

—*Ecclesiastes 4:12*

Our culture holds being independent and self-sufficient as its highest ideals. We celebrate the person who is able to go it alone, pull themselves up by their bootstraps, and succeed without help from anybody else. While on the surface this may seem admirable and even heroic, is it at all realistic, and is it what God intended for us?

We are made for community. We are made to be with one another and to help and support each other. In other words, when it comes to faith, you don't earn a gold star by going it alone. Most of the time, it is our pride that gets in our way and prevents us from connecting anyway. It is not good for Christians to remain in isolation because, let's face it, life and faith are hard! It is so much nicer when you can do life with others. Two are certainly better than one, but what about three or more? That's not something to trifle with.

Rather than feeling ashamed when we need help from others, let us celebrate the chance to connect with another for a common purpose. Rather than digging our heels in and stretching ourselves to the point of almost breaking, let us rejoice in having the confidence to ask for help from our friends and neighbors, knowing that when we do so, we allow another person to be as Christ to us.

Wade in the Water

- When do I allow my pride to stop others from helping me?

- When would being supported by others be seen not as a weakness, but as a strength?

Daily Action

The early Christian communities relied on one another for assistance. Are there ways you can better aid your community or allow your community to support you? Brainstorm a list of ways, large and small, that you can help and be helped—and then go and do some of those things!

Guided Prayer

Father, You created us to help one another. Please place people in my life who remind me that I am a beloved and needed member of a bigger community. Amen.

You Gotta Have Faith

But also for this very reason, giving all diligence,
add to your faith virtue, to virtue knowledge,
to knowledge self-control, to self-control perseverance,
to perseverance godliness, to godliness
brotherly kindness, and to brotherly kindness love.

—2 Peter 1:5–7

It just takes a look at a magazine cover to see that we really love lists and how-tos. Maybe it's because the world is so big that breaking something down to bite-size chunks makes it easier to process—or maybe it's because we have pretty short attention spans and can be easily distracted! Either way, today's encouragement from Peter can be best described as "Eight Steps to Become a More Complete Christian."

At first glance, it would be easy to see this list as just items to check off, but there is more here. In the same way the Ten Commandments were not just an itemized set of "dos" and "don'ts," Peter has outlined what each of us is called to become—how we can be perfected. But there is a catch: These steps are only possible through the descent of the Holy Spirit. Before He embarked on His crucifixion and resurrection, Jesus promised that God would send His Holy Spirit as an advocate for us, one who supported and defended the infant Christian communities and is still with us today. The Holy Spirit gives us the means to add virtue, knowledge, self-control, perseverance, godliness, brotherly kindness, and love to our faith, thus fulfilling our role on earth as followers of Christ.

But notice that Peter does not start us out with love. We all begin in the same place—with faith. When we decided to take up our crosses and follow Jesus, each of us put on a mantle of faith, a complete trust and confidence in something bigger than ourselves.

Wade in the Water

- How are you completely rooted in your faith and where can you strengthen your roots?

- In what ways can you continue to develop positive character traits?

Daily Action

Set aside time today to just reflect on the word *faith*. In your journal, draw, doodle, or write your responses to the following questions: What does faith mean to you? What is faith in action? How has your faith changed as you continue along the journey?

Guided Prayer

Jesus, thank you for sending Your Spirit to dwell among us. May Your Spirit come to dwell inside of me and inspire me to reach new heights and cast aside limitations. Amen.

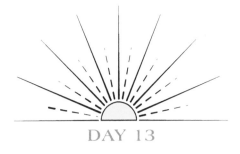

Made for a Purpose

You are all fair, my love, and there is no spot in you.

—*Song of Songs 4:7*

I remember it like it was yesterday: I was around 12 years old, staring at my reflection in the mirror, and the stream of negative dialogue in my mind was relentless. I had bad skin, buckteeth, and frizzy hair, my feet were too big, and my belly wasn't flat enough. I was not good enough for the world. I was so unlovable that my parents had divorced. I felt that God had made a mistake, and I was it.

It is very easy to see how the devil likes to use us against ourselves. He will look for every opportunity to encourage us to separate ourselves from others and from God. He is cunning, sly, and really has no need for new tricks, because all the old tricks work just fine. The devil was attacking the one fact that I was either choosing to ignore or had forgotten: that I was made perfectly in the image of God and that I was (and I am) loved unconditionally by the King of Kings.

Take a moment to read these words again and say them aloud to yourself: *I am made in the image of God.*

Friend, you are good enough. You have been made for a purpose that is yours alone. You are made in the image of God. He loves this world so much that He sent His Son to redeem it—and you—from the grips of the devil and his demons. God's love for you does not need a reason or justification. He loves you because He made you. God made you because He wants you to be happy with Him in heaven forever. Looks will come and go. Weight will go up and down. But through it all, God loves *you*.

Wade in the Water

- How does negative self-talk take away from the promise of God's unconditional love?

- What is your plan of counterattack when the devil puts his lies into your heart? Maybe you keep handy a collection of Bible verses to remind you of God's truth, or gather a trusted circle of friends who you know will pray for you when you need it most.

Daily Action

When you need a reminder of this truth that you are loved, and we all do from time to time, open your Bible to the book of Song of Songs (or Song of Solomon) and read some of the beautiful verses from the Creator to His creation.

Guided Prayer

Father in heaven, You knew who I was and what I was going to look like before the beginning of time. You made me as an individual and a unique creation, and I thank You for giving me life and breath. In Jesus's name, Amen.

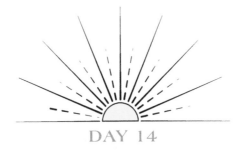

Better Together

And the Lord God said, "It is not good that man should be alone; I will make him a helper comparable to him."

—*Genesis 2:18*

I am an introvert by nature. There are times when I reflect on those early days of Creation and for a few moments think that Adam had it really good. I mean, there he was, surrounded by tons of animals, none of whom could talk back to him or argue with him, and yet God knew that Adam was incomplete. Even though Adam was not physically alone, he needed another of his kind with him in paradise. He needed a buddy. God created us for fellowship with one another. But making and maintaining friendships and relationships can be hard in the best of circumstances.

Factors like relocation, schedules, work, family, and health concerns can all get in the way of cultivating relationships, but we can always persevere and find work-arounds until we can come together again. Technology allows us to share laughs and celebrate milestones as little rectangles on a screen, and while it might not be as good as the real thing, it is not always terrible either. (How else can you celebrate a birthday with a friend halfway around the world in your pajamas?) We can choose to let distance and calendars keep us apart, or we can choose to come together using the means we have available. Sure, there is a feeling of uncertainty as we try to figure out how to be together in a new way and remember what it meant to laugh, cry, and love together. But what it comes down to is that it really is not good for us to be alone.

Wade in the Water

- When you need to be alone, what are you really craving or seeking?

- Do you find your relationships deepening or fracturing when you step away from them?

Daily Action

Is there someone in your life that you have not talked to in a while? Take five minutes today to pick up the phone and give them a call, not a video call, text, or email. Let them hear your voice and take the time to hear theirs.

Guided Prayer

Dearest Lord, forced time apart can bring out the best and the worst in each of us. Please give us opportunities to reconnect with one another in positive ways and to reflect on the ways each of us has grown through adversity. Amen.

Noble Friends Wanted

*As iron sharpens iron, so a man sharpens the
countenance of his friend.*

—Proverbs 27:17

In the ancient world, the sharpness of your tool was no joke. Whether used for farming or fighting, a dull instrument was not only dangerous but ineffective, and the process of sharpening the tool was time intensive and laborious. As with most things in life, the more time you spent making sure your tool was sound, the better off you would be when you had to use that tool.

This analogy can be taken a step further when it comes to our friendships. When we take the time to work at and develop our friendships, we are better for it. We are even more fortunate if we have at least one friend who will call us out when we are not living at our best and help us relocate the path to righteousness. I find it interesting that the above proverb uses the word *countenance*— we sharpen the faces of our friends by affecting their moods and emotions, but just as iron does not just make a knife look better, we are not just making cosmetic additions. We make our friends better by offering them words of encouragement, constructive criticism, or instruction, or by bearing their burdens. There are times when our friends will be receptive to the striking of the iron and there are

times when the reception will be a bit colder. There are times when
we are receptive to our friends' overtures, and times when we will
turn away from any advice or wisdom.

True friendship is persistent. It does not crumble when things
get hard or when the shine rubs off. Over time, we are all sharpened
by the ups and downs of genuine friendship, and we need each other
to ensure that we are kept sharp and ready for God to use.

Wade in the Water

- Who are the irons in your life that keep you sharp?

- In what ways can you be resistant to hearing criticism,
  especially from friends? How can you distinguish between
  genuinely negative criticism and constructive, potentially
  helpful advice?

Daily Action

Surrounding yourself with good friends will make you a better
person. Think about your friends list. Are there people around you
who do not bring out the best in you? Are those friendships worth
the investment of your time and talent, or would it be better to let
them go?

Guided Prayer

*Father in heaven, please give me opportunities to develop into a person
who can not only offer others criticism, encouragement, and instruction,
but also receive criticism, encouragement, and instruction from others. In
Jesus's name, Amen.*

A Good Name above All

*A good name is to be chosen rather than great riches,
loving favor rather than silver and gold.*

—*Proverbs 22:1*

I decided to spend one summer reading the novels written by Jane Austen. I remember going through an Austen phase in high school and I wanted to see if they still held value for me when reading them through older eyes. I can say for sure that the novels did change for me; in fact, they got better . . . and not just because of my girlhood crush on Mr. Darcy.

If you have ever read an Austen novel, the story typically focuses on a family dealing with poverty, where the only thing they really have going for them is the strength of their name. They tend to be truly good people who have fallen on hard circumstances. While the stories do end happily ever after for the virtuous characters, we can't say the same for those characters who are less than virtuous, whose misconduct easily becomes synonymous with their names (I'm looking at you, Willoughby!).

Our names are more than just our identity. They tell others about our integrity, our character, and our reputation. Material things are not bad in and of themselves, but they are inconstant—money can be here today and gone tomorrow, wealth can disappear in an instant, but your good name can last for generations. However, the reverse is also true in that a name that tarnished by word or deed can bring trouble to relationships due to a lack of trust or confidence. Those names may be better forgotten than remembered fondly.

Your name tells the world the kind of person you are, and that is so much more valuable than the balance in your bank account.

Wade in the Water

- What does your name mean to those around you? What do you think comes to mind when people hear your name?

- Which is more valuable to you: integrity or riches? Why?

Daily Action

Focus on integrity today. Strive to be a person that others can really count on. If you have a habit of breaking plans, decide today to honor your commitments. If you tend to run late, decide today to arrive five minutes early. Only give your word when you are able to keep it.

Guided Prayer

Jesus, people miles away from Galilee knew about the wonders and miracles done by You because of Your name. While I am not a miracle maker, grant me the ability to ensure that my name is one of integrity and trust to those who hear it. Amen.

A Wise Fool

Even a fool is counted wise when he holds his peace;
when he shuts his lips, he is considered perceptive.

—Proverbs 17:28

"God gave you two ears and one mouth for a reason." This was one of my mother's favorite sayings, and I remember as a kid thinking that was so weird. But as I go through life, I can really see the wisdom in this saying. What would the world around us really look like if we listened twice as much as we spoke?

In general, as humans, we talk a lot, and we like to hear our own voices repeated back to us. We are quick to share our opinions about anything and everything around us, and the more controversial the topic, the louder we want our side to be heard. Some of this might come down to the idea of belonging—we want to know exactly who is on our team and who is not—but other times it comes from a place of insecurity. Because we are not secure in ourselves, we seek our identity in what we believe in, be it our favorite sports team or a political leader. As Christians, however, we are not rooted in earthly things. We are rooted in what is above.

When we find our identity as followers of Christ, shouting our opinions from the rooftops doesn't seem all that important anymore.

We know where we belong, and we know to *Whom* we belong. We know that when God is for us, no one can be against us (Romans 8:31). There is a quiet confidence in the one who is able to keep their peace when others around them are warring. It's a confidence that I have to work at every day and can only do so through the grace of God.

Wade in the Water

- How can you offer unsolicited opinions without sounding pushy or overbearing?

- What is your biggest fear about remaining silent on a topic?

Daily Action

It is typically on social media or online that we truly allow ourselves to become fools. Today, offer a prayer before logging into your social media accounts or engaging in an Internet debate. Allow the Holy Spirit to speak for you, or encourage you to be silent.

Guided Prayer

Come, Holy Spirit, fill my heart with the knowledge and wisdom that I am safe and secure as a beloved child of God. Please inspire me to speak the words of life and, when needed, to keep silent and not be a fool to the world. Amen.

Keeping Your Lid On

*So then, my beloved brethren, let every man be swift
to hear, slow to speak, slow to wrath; for the wrath of
man does not produce the righteousness of God.*

—James 1:19–20

Early in our parenting journey, my husband and I resolved to learn how to be "positive parents." This parenting style is not characterized by saying yes all the time; it is more about respecting your children as separate creations and focusing on positive or logical consequences rather than negative or punitive ones.

In one of our first parenting classes, we learned about "flipping your lid." We've all been there. When life—or a situation—is spinning out of our control, you hit the point of no return on your emotions. The next thing you know, the veins in your neck are popping out, and you are screaming at the person standing before you. Our thinking brain, the neocortex, has been taken over by our mammalian brain, the limbic system, and all thinking has gone out of the window, and we are just a big, old bundle of emotions. We need healthy brain balance to keep everything running smoothly.

This is clearly not a new concept, as James cautioned the readers of his letter about the same thing. We are all called to hold our emotions in check, and that is best accomplished by listening carefully (avoiding assumptions), speaking carefully (choosing to lift up rather than tear down), and remaining slow to anger (keeping our lids on). When we are swift to hear, slow to speak, and slow to wrath, we avoid saying or doing something that we will later regret.

The best way to combat anger is through faith. We have to maintain the faith that God is in control and that all things will unfold according to His plan.

Stay swift to hear, slow to speak, and slow to wrath, and I would add one more: Let go and let God.

Wade in the Water

- Think back to the last time you flipped your lid. What was happening in your life that you felt you couldn't control?

- When we flip our lids, we usually have one of three reactions: fight, flight, or freeze. Which category do you fall into?

Daily Action

Flipping your lid does not have to become a reactionary experience. When you begin to feel yourself losing control, stop and recite Psalm 46:10: "Be still, and know that I *am* God." Repeat this as you breathe in and out slowly and from your core.

Guided Prayer

Father God, Psalm 103 reminds me that You are slow to anger. May I always remember that I am a reflection of Your nature and that I am also called to be slow to anger. In Jesus's name, Amen.

The Sam to Your Frodo

Therefore comfort each other and edify one another,
just as you also are doing.

—1 Thessalonians 5:11

In chapter four of Paul's first letter to the Thessalonians, Paul's words help them understand what will happen to their loved ones who died before the Second Coming of Jesus. Among the believers, there was a general fear that those who had already died would miss out on Christ's redemption. Paul reminds them that there is no need to worry because God has it all in His control, telling them that "the dead in Christ will rise first" (1 Thessalonians 4:16).

Paul continues the discussion in chapter five by reminding the Thessalonians of the amazing effect an encouraging word can have on a weary soul. Walking the path of Christianity is not an easy one, as told by J. R. R. Tolkien in the *Lord of the Rings* (LOTR) trilogy. This allegory of overcoming the weight of sin in our lives masterfully describes what the Christian life is about. We may think that taking up our crosses and following Christ will be a wide, easy road, but in reality it's a narrow, twisting path filled with things that would like nothing more than to destroy us.

Among all the LOTR characters, my favorite by far is Samwise Gamgee. Sam is not only best friends with Frodo Baggins, but at times Sam literally carries Frodo. Frodo is only able to accomplish his goal because of Sam's help. This is where your fellow believers come into play. Each of us is called to be a Sam to a Frodo, encouraging each other to keep going, even when it seems impossible. Sometimes that might even mean carrying your friend, physically or emotionally. Both Sam and the apostle Paul say that we need a friend to remind us that, as Sam says, "Even darkness must pass."

Wade in the Water

- Who are the people you can count on to offer an encouraging word in times of darkness? List them in your journal, then pick one and send them a note of gratitude.

- When was the last time you spoke a word of encouragement to someone else? What was the effect?

Daily Action

The act of building another up is not a one-and-done task. Choose to take part in varying means of building someone up, be it speaking words of encouragement, sharing personal sorrows, or praying a blessing over someone's day.

Guided Prayer

Jesus, we are children of the light, and we are called to speak truth, beauty, and goodness to one another. May the words that come from my mouth only serve to encourage other pilgrims on their journey. Amen.

No One Is Ever Alone

Now there stood by the cross of Jesus
His mother, and His mother's sister, Mary the wife
of Clopas, and Mary Magdalene.

—*John 19:25*

It's not easy to imagine ourselves standing at the foot of the cross, looking up at the bloodied and bruised body of our Savior, devoid of a life given up for us, but that is just what we are called to do. We do this not to dwell on what was a gruesome act, but because when we enter into the passion of Christ, we join with the apostle John and the women who remained with Jesus in their final act of great compassion. We join in an act of love.

Because we love the One who was crucified, the act of gazing upon His crucifixion reminds us just how far Jesus was willing to go out of love for us. This is the same love we are called to have for one another. As Jesus will never leave us alone, we must keep vigil for others in their suffering.

During Lent, our family contemplates the way of the cross. We reflect on the weight of the wood, how the thorns can scratch flesh, the sharpness of the nails driven through Jesus's hands and feet. We place ourselves there so that we will never forget what a great act of sacrifice Jesus made for us—an act we can never repay and were not worthy of to begin with. We reflect on the cross because Jesus's act of sacrifice opened the gates of heaven to us, and what was done will never have to be done again. This is the source of our joy. When we sit at the foot of the cross, we do not shed tears of sadness but tears of joy, we who are loved so much that Jesus was willing to die for us.

Wade in the Water

- How can the image of Christ crucified help you make different choices through the day?

- Do you find it difficult to think of the cross as a source of joy? How can you reflect on Jesus's sacrifice in a joyful way?

Daily Action

Spend some time today in contemplation of a cross. Let your mind reach out through time and space and sit at the foot of the cross with the apostle John and the women who loved Jesus. Imagine the smells around you, the heat on your skin, the noise of the crowd. Know that all of this was done just for you.

Guided Prayer

Lord Jesus, if I were the only person on earth, You would have given your life for my salvation just the same. Thank You for the gift of eternal life and for opening the gates of heaven to me. Amen.

DAY 21

Joy That Comes from Sorrow

Therefore you now have sorrow;
but I will see you again and your heart will rejoice,
and your joy no one will take from you.

—*John 16:22*

When Jesus speaks these words in the Gospel of John, He knows that He will soon break bread for the last time with His friends, and that at that meal one of the 12 apostles will betray Him. He will enter a grove of olives and pray to His father that this trial will pass over Him, begging so fervently that beads of blood form on His venerable face. Before noon the next day, He will be tried, sentenced, whipped, spit upon, ridiculed, mocked, and hanged on a wooden cross to die while the sun beats down upon His body.

And yet, with all of this knowledge swirling around in His mind, Jesus thinks not about Himself and what is about to pass, but about those who will be left behind. Rather than rush away or dwell on the negative, He takes this moment to comfort those around Him. Jesus's words of encouragement help us take to heart the lesson that sometimes we have to pass through pain before we enter into joy. We can't have Easter without Good Friday.

Jesus models for us the type of person we are called to be as Christians. In this passage, He gives us an example of what it means to not only sacrifice for others but bring them joy, even in the midst of sorrow. While it is true that we can't know the outcome of everything beforehand, we can still be like Jesus to one another, offering a kind word or a bit of encouragement to those who are suffering around us.

Wade in the Water

- Why do you think Jesus chose to model how to comfort in the midst of personal suffering?

- What benefit is there to sharing the suffering of someone else?

Daily Action

The next time a friend or acquaintance comes to you in suffering, take the time to not only listen to them attentively but also offer a kind word, even if it's uncomfortable or you are suffering too.

Guided Prayer

Holy Spirit, there are times when I want to shy away from those who are in pain. Please give me the fortitude to stand with them in their sorrow and speak the words of encouragement they need to hear. In Jesus's name, Amen.

Running for
the Crown

I can do all things through Christ who strengthens me.

—*Philippians 4:13*

Once upon a time, I decided to be a runner. I would see sleek and athletic people running effortlessly along Lake Michigan, and I wanted to be like them. So, I signed up to run the Chicago Marathon and trained with a local running club. With many marathon training plans, you run just short of a full marathon on training runs, but this one was different in that four weeks before the Chicago Marathon, we would train with a full 26.2 miles. It was decided that the training run would be the Milwaukee Marathon.

If you have ever run long distance, you know there is something surreal about the experience. You have to get comfortable with bodily functions happening at inopportune times, and you have to learn to silence the little voice inside your head that tells you what you are doing is ridiculous and that you can't do it. Right around mile 13, I could hear that little voice getting stronger, but then another voice cut through the clamor. It was a fellow marathoner, and he was evangelizing as he ran. During the time we kept pace together, he recited all of Philippians from memory. To this day, verse 4:13 is one I cling to when life gets hard.

I think that Paul must have been a runner because he uses a lot of running metaphors in his writing, but his words are not limited to just athletes. Alone we are nothing, but with Christ by our side we are superpowered. We can do all things through Christ because when we are aligned with His will great things happen. I am no longer a runner, and I was never sleek and athletic, but I did complete two marathons with Christ by my side.

Wade in the Water

- When things get difficult in your life, where do you turn first?

- When was the last time you did something hard? What did that feel like for you?

Daily Action

When we are faced with hard things, we tend to run away or avoid them. Rather than running away from a hard conversation, workout, project, or performance, remind yourself that you *can* do hard things with Christ to strengthen you.

Guided Prayer

Father God, You have created us for greatness, but we cannot accomplish it alone. Thank You for sending Your Son to walk among us and be that extra strength we need, especially when things get hard. Amen.

"Hey, I'll See Ya Later"

And God will wipe away every tear from their eyes;
there shall be no more death, nor sorrow, nor crying.
There shall be no more pain.

—Revelation 21:4

The phone call came the day after Thanksgiving. Our family had only been in California for just over a month, having moved far away from all of our extended family. I remember wondering who would be calling so early in the morning. I felt the bed shift as my husband padded downstairs to answer the phone, and I remember the heavy tread of his footsteps as he reentered the room. He sat down next to me on the bed, and with eyes glistening, stated plainly, "Your mother died last night."

She was a longtime smoker, and a heart attack had taken her while she slept. For the longest time, I carried with me a fear that the same thing would happen to me, and it is still a concern that creeps up from time to time. We were fortunate enough to have my mom visit right after we settled in California, and she was able to do all the things she had always wanted to do: see the Hollywood sign, eat at Roscoe's Chicken and Waffles, and dip her toes in the Pacific.

I remember my last words to her being ones of joy, as she wanted to know all about our first Thanksgiving in California. We ended the call as we always did, with the promise, "Hey, see ya later." This is a phrase I have adopted as my own. There are no "goodbyes" for me, just "See ya later." I was fortunate enough to have not only those words of closure with my mom but also the faith in knowing that Christ has conquered death for us. So, while our conversation is a little overdue, I'm looking forward to the moment I will, indeed, see her again.

Wade in the Water

- How is God's promise of no more death, sorrow, or crying meaningful to you?

- What phrase would you most like to be remembered for?

Daily Action

The practice of memento mori is one of remembering your death. It comes from the idea that we are all going to die and that it is best to remember that in our daily actions. Meditate on John Donne's sonnet "Death, Be Not Proud," and journal what is revealed to you through this poem.

Guided Prayer

Lord Jesus, the thought of death is scary, but it is also a part of living a full life. Please help me treasure my time here on earth, living my life to the fullest until You decide to call me home.

From Suffering to Glory

For I consider that the sufferings of this present time are not worthy to be compared with the glory which shall be revealed in us.

—Romans 8:18

We love comfort. We want our silky PJs, our shoes with gel inserts, our sheets made with 500-thread-count Egyptian cotton. We seek comfort, especially in our faith, and reject anything that gets in the way of our comfort, including suffering. Suffering, though uncomfortable, is a part of life; yet we try to avoid it at all costs.

When we first become believers, it's hard to fathom that suffering can be part of the deal. Christ makes all things new; why would He make suffering part of the faith? For new believers, that first encounter with suffering can be enough to turn away and go back to what's comfortable. The truth is, in taking up our crosses to follow Christ, we do not rid our lives of all problems. In fact, we may inherit new ones as we love those who do not agree with us or work to give Christ priority in our lives. These problems, at times, are much bigger than what we can handle on our own, but thankfully, we don't have to. As Christians, we are called to face temptations, tribulation when our faith is questioned, and persecution when we affirm our identities in Christ.

When we embrace the suffering in our lives, we better align ourselves with Christ and with other believers for whom suffering is a daily occurrence and not a temporary annoyance—those who are unable to gather because of war or who live where being a Christian is illegal. Paul reminds us that in suffering we can begin to let go of what ties us to earth and fix our eyes on heaven. God never allows us to suffer without a purpose. It is up to us to accept the cross offered to us, carry it bravely, and allow God to work within us.

Wade in the Water

- What habits or parts of your life have you been able to shed thanks to suffering?

- How does facing our suffering tie us more closely to Christ?

Daily Action

Reflect on the last time you were really suffering, and write about it in your journal. How do you think God could have used that suffering to His glory? What can you take away from this experience?

Guided Prayer

Lord Jesus, You faced physical suffering on earth to bring us heavenly glory. Please help me see that my suffering on earth is not only temporary but can also be used for good. Amen.

Letting Go of My Burdens

Come to Me, all you who labor and are heavy
laden, and I will give you rest . . .
For My yoke is easy and My burden is light.

—Matthew 11:28, 30

The muscle ache of physical labor is familiar, but what about the aches and pains caused by the burdens in our minds? We often struggle with a mental load of never-ending checklists, decisions, schedules, and obligations. How many of us have lain awake in bed, staring at the ceiling, trying to recall what we might have forgotten to do that day or what needs doing tomorrow?

Jesus's antidote to our burdens is to just come to Him. He does not have a multistep plan to execute or a complicated series of dos and don'ts to follow. He just tells us to come, give our burdens to Him, and rest in Him. Jesus is asking us to trust Him. If I can trust that Jesus can turn water into wine, I can trust Him to work a miracle in my own life to relieve some of the mental load that I bear.

When we let others in and trust that they will complete the tasks before them, we release our hold on the illusion of control, allowing God to work more freely within us. In empowering my children to make choices and deal with logical consequences, I am helping them become more responsible individuals. In sharing responsibilities with my husband, I am reinforcing the promises we made on our wedding day. When I find my trust in Jesus to work through those around me, I will find that it is truly well with my soul.

Wade in the Water

- What burdens are you currently carrying? Make a list in your journal.

- What is the worst that could happen if you let others carry some of your mental load?

Daily Action

Visualize the cross. Imagine setting your burdens at the foot of the cross, where Jesus is waiting with open arms. Next, take a look at your list from above and see what burdens you can share with those who love you.

Guided Prayer

Father God, You sent Your Son to us so we would never have to carry our burdens alone. Grant me the grace to allow Jesus to work through others to bear my load. In Jesus's name, Amen.

Failure Is Not an Option

My flesh and my heart fail; but God is the strength of my heart and my portion forever.

—*Psalm 73:26*

Growing up, one of my favorite movies was *Apollo 13*. I was a kid who loved all things space, and I was fascinated by the space program. I especially loved Ed Harris's performance as flight director Gene Kranz. Even if you are not familiar with the film, there is a good chance that you are familiar with Kranz's iconic line, delivered after the incident that launched the real-life Apollo 13 into the annals of history: "Failure is not an option."

Although the line was written for the movie, it is a statement of fact. If they failed, the astronauts would die. This line is what the NASA engineers needed to hear to keep them focused on the problem at hand. It is also the promise that God makes to each of us as His children. People will fail you. Your body will fail you. Friends, jobs, and dreams will all fail you.

In the above verse, the psalmist gives us the plain truth: God will never fail you. For our God, failure is never an option. We can see this played out in the whole of human existence. After the flood, God promised to never again destroy the earth. However, he knew that his creation would fail Him time and time again, so what did God do? He sent his Son, the rescuer, to save us, ransom us, and redeem us. God knew from the beginning that we would never be able to make it on our own, and that a sacrifice of His only begotten Son was the solution.

God never fails. In God we find our strength and our inheritance. We find the rock on which our hearts rely, a rock that will never be eroded by wind and rain but will stand forever.

Wade in the Water

- In what ways has God shown you that He will never fail you?

- Think about times or things that appeared to be failures but turned out to be blessings. How might God have been working in these situations?

Daily Action

People fail one another. Reflect on a time when you failed to keep your word or let down someone who was counting on you. Reach out, ask for forgiveness, and make amends.

Guided Prayer

Father in heaven, You are my rock, the one thing in life I can unfailingly count on. Thank You. In Jesus's name, Amen.

Healed by His Stripes

But He was wounded for our transgressions, He was bruised for our iniquities; the chastisement for our peace was upon Him, and by His stripes we are healed.

—*Isaiah 53:5*

O f all the Old Testament prophecies, this chapter from the prophet Isaiah most clearly lays out what the Redeemer would do for His beloved creation; however, this was not at all what the people of the time expected of their Messiah. For the people of Judea, the Messiah would be a king from the line of David, arriving on the scene with pomp and circumstance and full of glory. He would triumph over the foes of Israel, establishing His kingdom on Earth. He would be anointed with holy oils and would be a wise, noble king. He would be a servant of God who would build God's kingdom for all eternity and would have abilities and act in moral judgment (though he would not *be* God). Jesus didn't do any of that, however. He entered the world lowly, humbly, and quietly—as quietly as one can with a chorus of angels announcing a birth. He is God incarnate; a King to rule not on earth, but a Servant to open the gates of heaven. Despite the writings of the prophets, to the people of Judea, there was no way Jesus could be the Messiah. And yet He is.

Jesus's life and ministry are filled with examples of not acting as a king "should"; however, His final act was something even more radical: He sacrificed Himself for the betterment of all humankind. He gave His body and spirit up for you and me. Because of the actions of Adam and Eve, we were barred from the gates of heaven, but Jesus atoned for our sins so we could enter anyway. Our sins are the bruises on His body. They are the thorns on His head. By these wounds, we get a chance at heaven.

Wade in the Water

- In what ways was Jesus a suffering servant while on earth?

- The idea that Jesus suffered for our sins can be a difficult one to process. Have you ever taken on discomfort or suffering to help make a loved one's situation better? What was the outcome?

Daily Action

Healing from our wounds requires us to acknowledge where we are most hurting. Our wounds can be physical, mental, or emotional. Today, take stock of where you are in need of healing. Take steps to care for your well-being.

Guided Prayer

Lord Jesus, I am a sheep who sometimes goes astray. Thank You for always coming to look for me and for carrying me back to You. Amen.

Be Strong and Courageous

Be strong and of good courage; do not be afraid,
nor be dismayed, for the Lord
your God is with you wherever you go.

—*Joshua 1:9*

Fear is powerful and controlling. Fear is persuasive. It can convince us to decide one way or another. Fear can influence where we live, where our kids go to school, who we interact with. On one hand, fear can be protective, and certain fears have come to us over time to keep us from circumstances that might harm us. Fear of snakes? Keeps you away from venomous snakes. Fear of heights? Good way to prevent a deadly fall. Fear of sharks? Keeps you from going too deeply into the ocean. Some fears can keep us safe, but other fears hold us back. It's those irrational fears that we have to be most aware of.

How many of us limit our potential because we are afraid? We are afraid to pursue our dreams because we might fail. We are afraid to move to a new state because our familiar and comfortable will no longer be familiar and comfortable. We are afraid to share our true selves on social media because we fear getting fewer likes. But the ironic thing is, in not trying, we have already failed. Fear is a self-fulfilling prophecy.

I love how God simply states, "Do not be afraid." He's not suggesting; He's not asking. He is commanding us not to fear. As long as the Lord is with us and we are doing His will, there is nothing to be afraid of. So, the next time you feel the Spirit tugging at your core about something God wants you to do—be it offering a meal to an unhoused person, talking to a stranger about your faith, or moving to a new place—be not afraid, for God is with you.

Wade in the Water

- Think of a time when God was calling you to do something but fear got in the way. What was the result?

- How can Joshua 1:9 help you overcome your fears?

Daily Action

Open your Bible to the book of Joshua and highlight every time you see the phrase "Be strong, and of good courage" (or any variation of this phrase). When you need a reminder, refer back to Joshua to remind yourself to be strong and courageous.

Guided Prayer

Father God, Joshua knew that he was to enter the Promised Land, and yet he still needed to be reminded not to fear. Please send Your Spirit to remind me to be brave and courageous because You are with me. In Jesus's name, Amen.

Reason, Season, Lifetime

To everything there is a season, a time for every
purpose under heaven ... A time to weep, and a time
to laugh; a time to mourn, and a time to dance.

—*Ecclesiastes 3:1, 4*

Just before my 30th birthday, we moved to California. I was a stay-at-home mom with two little kids, and one of the first things I did was join a group for mothers of young children with a twofold goal: My kids would make friends, and I would make friends. This group also included a dedicated, experienced mother who would speak and teach, and would basically have us walking out of the room knowing that we were good moms. It was during one of these teaching sessions that I first heard this statement about friendships: "Some friendships are formed for a reason, some friendships are formed for a season, and some friendships are formed for a lifetime." It has always reminded me of this verse from Ecclesiastes, not just because of its rhythm but because of its focus on the seasonal and cyclical nature of friendship. In that room I met women who would become my sisters, not only in Christ but in life.

When we begin a new friendship or relationship, we have no idea if it is for a reason, season, or lifetime. We may only find out the purpose of that friendship after something changes in our lives. It could be a hardship, death, marriage, divorce, birth of a child, or move across the country. In the end, people come into and out of our lives, and rather than mourning the change, let's celebrate because of what was, is, and is to come. While I can't see those women in person as easily anymore, the friendships that started for a reason and developed over many seasons have become lifetime connections.

Wade in the Water

- Look back over your friendships, especially ones that have ended. How and why were those friendships forged? What did you gain from them?

- How does recognizing your friendships as a "reason," "season," or "lifetime" help you fully appreciate each connection?

Daily Action

Write a letter to a friend expressing your gratitude and appreciation for their friendship. Find some nice stationery or just grab some notebook paper. Let the Spirit guide your words and drop it into the mailbox.

Guided Prayer

Dearest Lord, we tend to avoid change, especially in friendships. Help me embrace change as an opportunity for growth rather than something to mourn. Through Christ, Amen.

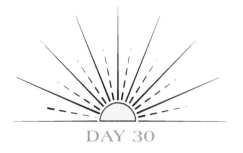

Your Body Is a Temple

*Or do you not know that your body is the temple
of the Holy Spirit who is in you, whom you have from
God, and you are not your own? For you were
bought at a price; therefore glorify God in your body
and in your spirit, which are God's.*

—*1 Corinthians 6:19–20*

We all have those trigger spots—those areas of our bodies that our eyes zero in on when we are getting dressed, brushing our teeth, or just going through our days. In these moments, we can end up on a downward spiral of negative self-talk. We might wish away our freckles, our acne, or those gray hairs that tend to multiply in the night.

All around us are messages about our bodies. We are called to be body positive—to celebrate what we have—or to be body neutral and just accept that the body is the body. A common thought in first-century Corinth is one that still floats around today: The body is nothing but a shell, and the spirit is what's important. This is called "gnosticism," and Paul considered it so off the mark that he addressed it in his letter to the church at Corinth.

God did not create us to be spirits separate from the body, because if that was His intent, that is all we would be. Rather, God created us to be spirits in communion with our bodies, with the body and spirit as one in Christ Jesus. Our bodies are temples to the Holy Spirit, so we use them to honor God. Our bodies belong to God, and they are made to glorify God in all that we say and do. God created our bodies to be most efficient when we make good choices about food, rest, and movement, so we can do the good things that He has called us to do.

Wade in the Water

- Think about your body trigger points. How can those areas be used to glorify God?

- Reflect on the idea that your body and spirit are one in Jesus Christ. What does that mean for you and how you might live your life?

Daily Action

Find a sticky note or slip of paper and write "I am a temple of God" on it. Stick it on a mirror you use every day (or write directly on the mirror with a dry-erase marker) for a daily reminder of your body's value in Christ.

Guided Prayer

Father God, I honor You with my actions, thoughts, words, and body. Forgive me for my past indiscretions and may I walk forward in Your glory. Through Christ, Your Son, Amen.

Just as Your Soul Prospers

*Beloved, I pray that you may prosper in all things and
be in health, just as your soul prospers.*

—*3 John 1:2*

I
n the opening of his third letter, John shares a hope for its
recipient, a man named Gaius. From the tone of the letter, we
can get the idea that Gaius is a warmhearted, generous individual, and John clearly wants to commend him for that: He
shares with Gaius his hope that his physical life is a reflection of his
spiritual life.

We live in a society that treasures physical appearance above
all else. Take a look at magazine covers or targeted ads or even your
social media feed. We want to look good for others, no matter what
we feel like inside, and others want us to look good for them. We
can do a lot to make our physical bodies look good, but is it all a
facade? Are we putting in time and effort to make ourselves look
good on the outside while neglecting our broken insides? Do our
physical bodies truly match our spiritual selves, or do we project to
the world that all is fine even when it is not?

Since we know that our bodies and our spirits are not separated, our physical selves can be a great indicator of how our spiritual selves are doing. Are you feeling run-down, uninspired, or just plain meh? Maybe it's time for a spiritual check-in. Are there obstacles between you and God? Are you carrying a burden that you need to lay at His feet? Do not be afraid to seek help from others; after all, there are many pilgrims on this journey, and we are here to help one another.

Wade in the Water

- What would it mean for you to hear John's words prayed over you? How would a prayer like that make you feel?

- How can you break free of the limited view of physical health and appearance that our society champions?

Daily Action

Read 3 John in its entirety (it's not long, I promise!). In your journal, compare the examples of Gaius and Diotrephes. Which of these two is reflective of who you are now?

Guided Prayer

Lord Jesus, in You may my body prosper in all things and be healthy as my soul prospers and is healthy. Amen.

Eat, Drink, and Be Merry!

Therefore, whether you eat or drink, or whatever you do, do all to the glory of God.

—*1 Corinthians 10:31*

I f food were a love language, it would definitely be mine. I love food. I love trying new foods. I love old, familiar comfort foods. I love cooking food and trying new recipes. To me, food is joy. It's a gift from God that we are meant to embrace, love, nourish ourselves with, and share with others. However, my love of food and slowing metabolism (hello, 40s!) have meant having to relearn some habits and become more mindful about my eating choices.

In the Old Testament, the Israelites are given guidelines about foods that are clean or unclean. The clean foods are okay to eat, and the unclean foods are not. There are also rules as to what foods can be combined with other foods. Members of the Jewish faith who keep a kosher house adhere to these commandments today as they have for thousands of years.

When Jesus came on the scene, he did something radical for the time. In the Gospel according to Mark, Jesus declares all foods clean, saying that the "unclean" things that go into our hearts, not the food that enters our stomachs, are what we really have to be concerned about.

For many of us who have grown up in the United States, diet culture is part and parcel with who we are. We train ourselves to moralize our food choices, categorizing foods as "good" or "bad" when really they are morally neutral—and gifts from God. We feel shame when another diet fails or when we "cheat." Rather than idolizing the diets of the day, let's try eating and drinking while giving glory to God.

Wade in the Water

- What is your relationship with food?

- Have you ever used food to reward or soothe yourself? How might your life change if you went to God for rewards or support instead?

Daily Action

When you sit down to your next meal, rather than rushing though a table blessing, really take a moment to stop and celebrate God's love for you through His gift of food.

Guided Prayer

Bless me, O Lord, and these thy gifts, which I am about to receive from thy bounty. Through Christ, our Lord. Amen.

Fully Satisfied

And Jesus said to them, "I am the bread of life.
He who comes to Me shall never hunger, and he who
believes in Me shall never thirst."

—John 6:35

"I am who I am."

We first hear God use the name "I AM" for Himself in the book of Exodus, when Moses meets God in Midian, where Moses has fled after killing the Egyptian. Moses encounters a bush that is burning but not consumed, and there we hear the name of God: I AM. Moving forward through time (and in our Bibles), in John's Gospel we meet Jesus, the Miracle Maker. While the other Gospels talk about Jesus's lineage and birth, comings and goings, relationships, and a, John's Gospel focuses on the divinity of Christ, the loaves and fishes, so to speak. In John's Gospel we hear about *why* we should believe in Christ. John's Gospel is written for those who already believe that Jesus is the Messiah, and it gives us more insight into Jesus as the Son of God.

One unique thing about John's Gospel is that it contains seven "I am" statements. These declare who the person of Jesus is and what He was sent to earth to do. We know that Jesus is all about relationships. He wants to know and love us personally, and this is best expressed in the "I am" statements. Not only is He recalling what Moses learned from God the Father, but He is also sharing what God the Father wants for us and is giving to us through God the Son.

When the Israelites were wandering for years in the desert, God gave them the gift of bread from heaven (manna) to sustain them until they could enter the land of Canaan. In the person of Jesus, God sends His Son as the bread of life to sustain us until we can enter heaven.

Wade in the Water

- What does it mean to hunger and thirst in your spiritual life?

- Why do you think Jesus decides to use bread for His first "I am" statement?

Daily Action

Grab your highlighter and your Bible! Open up to the Gospel of John and locate and highlight the seven "I am" statements. What do these statements reveal to you about God's character and how do they reflect His love for you?

Guided Prayer

Jesus, thank You for nourishing me in my mind, body, spirit, and life. May all I have praise Your holy name. Amen.

Miles to Go

For bodily exercise profits a little, but godliness is profitable for all things, having promise of the life that now is and of that which is to come.

—1 Timothy 4:8

The community where we live surrounds a lake. This should not shock me, coming from "the land of 10,000 lakes"; however, I am surprised at how much this little lake delights me and what it has become for me. There are two paths that go around the lake, one for bikes and one for walking and running, and starting the day with a loop around the lake is good not only for my physical life but also for my spiritual life.

As I move forward step-by-step around the loop, I use the time to converse with God. This is our time together, free from distractions and to-do lists. Sometimes my prayers are extemporaneous, just me rattling off whatever is on my heart or mind at that moment. Other times I like the more structured prayers of my faith, allowing the ancient words to fade into the background as I meditate on the mysteries of my Savior's life. Feeling my heart pump blood through my body reminds me of the gift of life that I, every morning, get to experience. I wave to familiar faces: neighbors out walking their dogs, the lady from down the street in her motorized wheelchair. We are all out together, enjoying the beauty of God's creation.

By the end of the loop, I have traveled about 1.5 miles (2.4 km); however, that physical distance is unmatched by the connection that I've made with my Savior that morning, a connection that will support, encourage, and delight me throughout my day.

Wade in the Water

- What is "godliness," and how is that produced in a person?

- 1 Timothy 4:8 can be misinterpreted as a reason not to exercise. How do you think some draw this conclusion?

Daily Action

Add a bit of prayer to your exercise routine. Whether saying a prayer when you begin, when you finish, or as a way to mark time throughout, work both your physical and spiritual body today.

Guided Prayer

Lord Jesus, grant me the grace to develop my spiritual life as much as (or more than) my physical life. In Your name, Amen.

Pursuing What Is Good

*Now we exhort you, brethren, warn those who
are unruly, comfort the fainthearted, uphold the weak,
be patient with all. See that no one renders evil for
evil to anyone, but always pursue what is good both for
yourselves and for all.*

—1 Thessalonians 5:14–15

It seems like not a day goes by without another culture war popping up to divide the faithful. Women teaching in the church? Check. Supporting one political candidate over another? Check. Life choices accepted by the church? Check. Every day is another opportunity for us to fall into one argument or another.

Culture wars are not new for Christianity. Many of Paul's writings in the New Testament are directed to differing groups in the area and are used as gentle reminders of what the faith is and what it is not. The first letter to the church at Thessalonica is written to a group of new believers, a mix of both Jews and gentiles. Paul's letter serves as one of encouragement for the new believers, but also as an instructional tool: What should a Christian do when things begin to go awry? I love how Paul, after giving some specific examples, ends with the phrase "Pursue what is good both for yourselves and for all." What is good for ourselves and one another? Jesus.

We are followers of Jesus and therefore we should imitate Him. Jesus was not afraid to speak the truth—but He always shared the truth in love, and that is how it should be for us. We are all followers of Christ coming from different churches and faith traditions, not unlike the different churches throughout the ancient world. Yet we have one thing in common: We are all redeemed by the cross. Friends, let us not allow culture wars to divide us; rather, let us remain united under the one who loved us so much that He died for us.

Wade in the Water

- Which Christian culture war is most distressing for you, and how can you disengage from it?

- What are some ways we can "pursue what is good" instead of "rendering evil for evil"?

Daily Action

Thank God every time you have the opportunity to practice the virtue of patience with someone in your life.

Guided Prayer

Dearest Jesus, You were sent to separate the faithful from the world, not to distance the faithful from Your heart. Please inspire my speech and actions to be one of unity, not division. Amen.

Let Us Wait upon the Lord

But those who wait on the Lord shall renew their strength; They shall mount up with wings like eagles, they shall run and not be weary, they shall walk and not faint.

—Isaiah 40:31

When I was a kid, one of my favorite Bible stories was about Samson and Delilah. Samson, a miracle baby, is set aside by his parents to be a Nazirite, serving God all the days of his life. This means he is supposed to abstain from wine and grapes, avoid the bodies of the dead, and never cut his hair and beard. As Samson grows, he develops unmatched physical and mental strength and is made a judge over the people of Israel. Then he meets Delilah and starts to make some poor choices. His love for Delilah takes over all reasoning in his life, and the enemies of Israel decide to use Delilah to take down Samson. They need to find out the secret of his strength to defeat this great protector of Israel. Samson tells Delilah that the secret is his long hair, hair that he has promised never to cut, and he allows Delilah to cut his hair. Having broken his promise to God, Samson loses his strength and is captured and imprisoned by the enemies of Israel.

This story made an impression on me because it highlights where our strength is found. We are not strong because of what we do or who we are; we are strong because we have the Lord. Our culture champions those who are able to go it alone, carve their own paths, and do things because of their strength, but we forget that we are only as strong as our faith. In the end, Samson does not grow strong again because his hair grows back. He grows strong again because he recognizes from Whom his strength comes and realizes how utterly dependent he is on God.

Wade in the Water

- In times of stress and/or weakness, what do you find comforting?

- When do you find yourself forgetting that God is the source of your protection and strength?

Daily Action

Think of two or three people in your life who are most vulnerable right now. Reach out and ask how they are doing and what you can do for them.

Guided Prayer

Lord God, thank You for Your awesome power and for the strength You give me to move forward with my mission here on earth. In Christ's name, Amen.

The Prayer Jar

*Be anxious for nothing, but in everything by prayer
and supplication, with thanksgiving, let your
requests be made known to God; and the peace of God,
which surpasses all understanding, will
guard your hearts and minds through Christ Jesus.*

—*Philippians 4:6–7*

I have a jar tucked into the back of my closet. It's not a fancy jar; it's made of plastic. But it is what the jar contains that is the treasure. Inside the jar are my prayers from over the years: little pieces of envelopes, notebook papers, newspapers, random scraps of paper all filled with my hopes, fears, petitions, worries, and anxieties, all written to God.

For the first part of our married life, my husband traveled a lot for work, and this meant that I was alone for many days during the month. This setup was fine until we had children. Not only did the physical and mental workload increase when we added little people to the mix, but the evil one found a perfect way to chip away at my faith and resolve by zeroing in on my deepest fears, like falling ill and leaving my small children unattended or rejection when reaching out to a new friend. Knowing the power of prayer and the power that God has over the evil one, I started my prayer jar. When something was on my heart to the point where it was affecting my day-to-day life, I would write it on a piece of paper and stick it into the jar. Once the prayer was in the jar, the stress and anxieties would melt away; I was filled with God's peace. Not only was the jar my way of casting my anxieties on Him (1 Peter 5:7), it was a physical way to let my requests be made known to God.

I've never looked back at the old prayers in that jar because, for me, the jar is not there to show me how God answers my prayers. It allows me to fully trust that God has everything in hand. I just need to have the strength to let go of what I am clinging to and give it to God.

Wade in the Water

- What fears or anxieties does the evil one like to use against you?

- How do you respond to the request "Be anxious for nothing"?

Daily Action

Create your own prayer jar. Find a simple vessel: a glass or plastic jar, an empty butter tub, etc. around your house. When worries and anxieties crop up, write them down, pray over them, and stick them in the jar, giving them to God.

Guided Prayer

Father in heaven, You already know what I need before I ask for it. Thank You for taking my worries and cares when I offer them to You. In Christ Jesus, Amen.

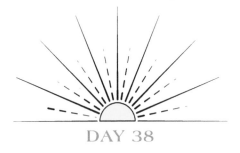

Dry Bones

*The hand of the Lord . . . set me down
in the midst of the valley; and it was full of bones . . .
"Then you shall know that I am the Lord,
when I have . . . brought you up from your graves."*

—*Ezekiel 37: 1, 13*

There are times when I feel very much like I am in exile, wandering around in the wilderness, lost and separated from God. I'll sit down with my Bible or get in a comfortable spot to pray, and I'll reach out to God, pleading and seeking, only to be faced with a desert. Like the prophet Ezekiel, I am staring down a desolate valley filled with piles and piles of dry bones. It's also right around this time that the evil one begins to whisper his lies in my ear: My faith is not strong enough; God really doesn't care about me; I'm all alone and I have always been alone.

And then the rattling starts. Those bones piled around me start to rattle and move and build and remind me that I am never alone, because God promised that I wouldn't be. It's easy to focus on and despair about the sheer number and dryness of the bones that compose our spiritual lives and completely miss that God keeps His promises.

God promises life and wholeness and family. He promises us that we shall have His Spirit and through that Spirit we shall live, not because of something we have done, but because we are His people. We belong to Him. We are His beloved.

Spiritual dryness is not something we can choose to avoid, nor is it something for us to fear. Rather than letting our minds tell us that God has abandoned us, let us choose to listen for the rattle and remember that God will never leave us behind. When we are parched, dry, and in need of God's Spirit, let us not despair but turn to drink from the well of the living water offered by Christ.

Wade in the Water

- When you notice that you are in a state of spiritual dryness, do you draw closer to God or pull away? Why?

- How does your outlook change if you view spiritual dryness as a gift rather than a burden?

Daily Action

Spend 5 to 10 minutes today in contemplative prayer, just reflecting and focusing on God. Do not enter into this spiritual space with a plan of action; rather, let the Spirit of God breathe into you and bring you forth from the grave.

Guided Prayer

Father in heaven, let the rattling of the dry bones around me recall Your promise of life with You. Breathe new life into me, so I may do Your will. Amen.

United in Christ

*Now I plead with you, brethren, by the name
of our Lord Jesus Christ, that you all speak the same
thing, and that there be no divisions among
you, but that you be perfectly joined together in the
same mind and in the same judgment.*

—*1 Corinthians 1:10*

If the last few years had a theme, it would be division. We saw friends and families dividing and separating over political and social issues, decisions, and opinions in ways we might not have thought possible. We were asked to physically separate in an effort to decrease the effects of a global pandemic, meaning that many of us were separated from our Christian communities as well.

In many ways, the church at Corinth was dealing with the same issues we see today. The people of Corinth were developing preferences for one teacher over another, and while there is no problem with having a preference, it does become a problem when that preference leads to a schism.

We all have preferences. Some of us like organ music for worship, while others prefer electric guitar and drums. Some want to be inspired by a dynamic preacher, while some yearn for the peace and silence of quiet contemplation. Preferences are perfectly normal and part of human behavior, but when our preferences lead to isolation and rejection of those who do not share our preferences, we lose sight of what Jesus taught us.

Yes, Jesus did say that He came to earth to divide (Luke 12). He came to divide us from our selfish desires, from our injustices toward one another, from our sinful ways. Jesus came to divide us from a fallen world so that we could go out into that same world to share His love and peace. As Christians, we are united in Christ. Some of us are Catholic, some Evangelical, others Lutheran, Methodist, Baptist, or members of the Church of Jesus Christ of Latter-day Saints. Our dogmas are not what define us. We are siblings in Christ, for all time.

Wade in the Water

- Describe the feelings that come up when you find yourself in a divided community.

- What are some ways that we can bring folks together, be it in church, at work, or in school?

Daily Action

Seek to unite with someone from whom you feel divided. It could be someone in person or someone on social media. Focus on what connects you rather than divides you. Offer an olive branch of peace.

Guided Prayer

Lord Jesus, there are days when I feel like Your church is divided from itself. Help me be a connecting point that reminds us all that we are one in You. Amen.

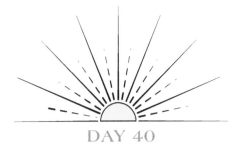

The Lights Don't Lie

*But if we walk in the light as He is in the light,
we have fellowship with one another, and the blood of
Jesus Christ His Son cleanses us from all sin.*

—*1 John 1:7*

In my teen years, the local YMCA would hold monthly dances for the teens in the community. The entry fee would be a few dollars and the dance was usually over by 10 p.m. The staff would change the multipurpose room into a dance floor, and the preferred decorating style of the time was to use a black light (ultraviolet light). We would walk into the space in our best neon-colored clothing, and we would start to glow . . . both in a good way and a bad way. You see, ultraviolet light makes colored pigments glow. It highlights the lint on your clothes and even the blotches left by the brighteners in your laundry detergent! There was nothing hidden from the effect of the black light.

That's exactly what light does. You can't hide anything in the light. Light reveals everything, both our good places and those that need improvement. When we keep things hidden from one another in fellowship, we are not being 100 percent honest with our friends, nor with ourselves—and a friendship not built on honesty is not much of a friendship at all. There is a temptation, especially when embarking on a new friendship, to only show the best parts of you and keep hidden the parts that are challenging or in need of support. But that is the goal of friendship and community—to support one another. All of us have things in our past we are not proud of. All of us have said things that no longer reflect who we are, and all of those things are forgiven by the blood of Jesus. Let the light of Christ reveal who you are to your friends and family without hiding.

Wade in the Water

- How is John's love for the Christian people evident in this verse?

- Why is truthful living so important in communities and friendships?

Daily Action

Take a flashlight and shine it in a place that rarely gets light. It might be under your bed or behind your dresser. Are there things that have been hidden from you or things that have been lost and are now found?

Guided Prayer

Father God, allow nothing of myself to remain hidden from those who love me and whom I love. In Jesus's name, Amen.

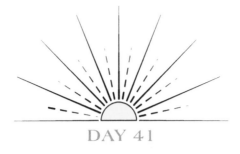

Asking vs. Assuming

Therefore, as the elect of God, holy and beloved, put on tender mercies, kindness, humility, meekness, longsuffering; bearing with one another, and forgiving one another, if anyone has a complaint against another; even as Christ forgave you, so you also must do.

—*Colossians 3:12–13*

I spent a series of weeks working with a life coach when I was trying to fully discern what direction the Lord was encouraging me to go in. During one of our meetings, the topic of forgiveness and saying "I'm sorry" popped up, and he shared an insight with me that was mind-blowing. At its root, an apology is an argument, which is why defense of the Christian faith is called "apologetics." Therefore, when you are making an apology, you are really presenting an argument as to *why* you should be forgiven. You are not actually asking for forgiveness. In saying "I'm sorry," we are expecting the response of forgiveness without really asking for forgiveness.

This was such a reversal of thought for me. I was not really asking for forgiveness; I was assuming forgiveness. Since that meeting, when I am at fault in an interaction or when my kids find themselves in conflict, we begin the process of reconciliation with "Please forgive me for . . ." In his letter to the church at Colossus, Paul reminds us of the qualities that we have because we are counted among the elect, God's followers. In choosing to follow Christ, we hold ourselves to a different standard than those who have not yet met our Divine Master. In asking someone for forgiveness instead of simply apologizing when we have wronged them, not only do we acknowledge what we did but we no longer assume that forgiveness will come; there is a risk that forgiveness will *not* be given. It is a humbling act that relies on the mercy and kindness of another person, and it is just what we are called to do as followers of Christ.

Wade in the Water

- What is the difference between asking for forgiveness and assuming forgiveness?

- Which of the qualities that Paul outlines is the easiest for you? The hardest?

Daily Action

Today, when you make a mistake (because we all do), begin your reconciliation with "Please forgive me for . . ." rather than "I'm sorry for . . ." How does changing the phrasing change your feelings about reconciliation?

Guided Prayer

Lord Jesus, please forgive me for the times when I have withheld forgiveness from another out of pettiness or spite. Help me always seek reconciliation. Amen.

Prayer Changes Everything

Confess your trespasses to one another, and pray for one another, that you may be healed. The effective, fervent prayer of a righteous man avails much.

—*James 5:16*

History is full of people who start out one way and then become something different. Saul was a brutal killer of Christians until he was knocked off his horse and blinded. He converted to Christianity, took the name Paul, and became a fervent disciple of Christ. Watching the death of Christians was a form of entertainment for the Roman Empire before the conversion of Emperor Constantine the Great. Even the actor John Wayne is alleged to have had a full conversion to Christianity just before his death in 1979. But one of my favorite conversion stories is that of Augustine of Hippo, thanks to the prayers of his mother, Monica of Hippo.

Monica was a Christian; her son and husband were not. Augustine's father was a pagan and taught his son that worldly wants and desires were of the utmost concern in life. Everything that one could want was out there; you just had to take it. Augustine did. He stole, he took many lovers, he fathered a child outside of marriage, he drank to excess—he truly lived each day as if it was his last day. All the while, his mother prayed for him and for her husband, and because of Monica's prayers, both her son and husband turned from their ways and began following Christ.

Augustine went on to become one of the church's greatest teachers and thinkers, and his works are still widely read and referenced today. It was because his mother wanted so much more for him, and she knew that true conversion could only come from God. So don't ever think your prayers are powerless. Prayer changes everything.

Wade in the Water

- Is it easier to pray when life is going well or when life is challenging? Why?

- Why does James say that in confessing to and praying for others, *we* are healed?

Daily Action

Experiment with different prayer postures today. If you normally pray while seated, try standing or kneeling or even lie down prostrate on the ground. If you pray indoors, head outside for your conversation with God. Step out of your normal!

Guided Prayer

Father God, I know that prayer has power, and yet I sometimes forget. I believe that You do hear and answer my prayers. Please help my unbelief. In Jesus's name, Amen.

Called Out of Darkness

*But you are a chosen generation, . . . His own special
people, that you may proclaim the praises of Him who
called you out of darkness into His marvelous light.*

—*1 Peter 2:9*

As Christians in the Western world, it's hard to
imagine ever being rejected because of your faith.
According to a Pew research study published in 2020,
at the time of this writing, around 70 percent of
Americans classify themselves as Christian. It is not abnormal to see
Christian images or traditions woven into secular media, television
shows, even into political campaigns. But things were very different
for first-century Christians in the Holy Land.

Once an individual made the decision to follow Christ, they
were no longer Roman citizens because they rejected the Roman
mandate to worship Caesar. They were no longer followers of
Judaism because they believed the Messiah had come in the person
of Jesus. In accepting Christ, they cast off their old identity in favor

of a new one. When *we* accept Christ, we do the same. But what is that new identity?

Peter gives us the answer simply: We belong to God. We were called out of darkness into the light. We are orphans who now have a father, castoffs who are children of a king. Walking the path of Christianity is not an easy one, but we keep in mind that our God rescued us and wants the best for us. People will fail us, but God never will. In Christ we are accepted, valuable, and forgiven.

Wade in the Water

- Explain Peter's description of God's people in your own words.

- What has God done for you that is praiseworthy?

Daily Action

God did not just come to save us out of sin, but to be a community of His chosen people. Make a plan to invite a few fellow Christians into your space for fellowship, community, or a meal.

Guided Prayer

Father in heaven, I praise You because I am fearfully and wonderfully made. Thank You for calling me out of darkness and into light. In Christ's name, Amen.

Whom Do You Love the Least?

Let brotherly love continue. Do not forget to entertain strangers, for by so doing some have unwittingly entertained angels. Remember the prisoners as if chained with them—those who are mistreated—since you yourselves are in the body also.

—Hebrews 13:1–3

"Love one another; as I have loved you" (John 13:34). As a chosen people, belonging to Christ, we are held to a higher standard than others and we have specific roles to play in God's plan for humanity. One of the biggest ones involves this idea of love. In the Gospel according to John, Jesus gives us the directive to love one another, with Him as the example. How did Jesus love us? He loved us to death. Does that mean that we are called to die for one another if needed? Maybe. At minimum, it does mean that we should seek the best for one another.

Born in 1897, Dorothy Day was an American journalist, social activist, and anarchist who converted to Catholic Christianity and became an advocate for the poor. She worked to support the working poor, immigrants, and people who society at large would have rather pushed to the margins. She wrote in one of her letters, "Our manifesto is the Sermon on the Mount, which means that we will try to be peacemakers." This phrase often comes into my mind exactly when I need the reminder, because love and peace tend to travel hand in hand.

We are a people of love and we are made for love. That love is not just reserved for those we personally care about, but also (and maybe especially) for those we may not particularly like or value. We are called to love our siblings in Christ *and* the stranger in our midst and the prisoner behind bars. We are called to love and serve one another as Christ loves and serves us.

Wade in the Water

- How can you love not just in theory but in action?

- In what ways are love and truth connected?

Daily Action

Call to mind someone you find very difficult to love. Pray that God allows you to see them through His eyes and opens your heart to love them as they are.

Guided Prayer

Lord Jesus, You came to free us all from the bondage of sin. Today, be with those who are imprisoned, both justly and unjustly, until they, too, are freed. Amen.

Discovering Unity

*There is one body and one Spirit, just
as you were called in one hope of your calling; one Lord,
one faith, one baptism; one God and Father
of all, who is above all, and through all, and in you all.*

—*Ephesians 4:4–6*

Every January, many of us in the Northern Hemisphere observe the "Week of Prayer for Christian Unity." Dating back to 1908, this is a week where Christians from all over the world observe a time of prayer for visible Christian unity, thereby moving us closer to Jesus's prayer at the Last Supper that we "all may be one" (John 17:21). If your church or group participates in the observance, your experience might look something like this: There are prayers vocalized during your weekly service about finding unity, an ecumenical celebration in which church leaders from the area come together to worship, and a general goal of finding and producing unity among all followers of Christ. But what if we are looking at things from the wrong angle? What if Christian unity is not something to be produced, but something that already exists? What if it's not missing, but we're just blind to it?

Unity among the peoples of Christ was already established once the work of Christ was completed on the cross. This is why God sent the Holy Spirit to dwell among us. We don't have to create unity, but we could do a better job of expressing it. Let's focus on what we have in common rather than allowing the evil one to sow seeds of division and cause us to dissolve into bickering, infighting or struggling against one another. When we come together in Christ, let's come together to lift up one another, pray for one another, support one another, and, yes, forgive one another.

Wade in the Water

- How would someone see the peace, unity, and love of Christ in you?

- What actions are required to discover unity rather than produce unity?

Daily Action

Look up the names that are used to describe the Holy Spirit. Which of those titles would you associate most with Christian unity? How can you better reflect Christian unity through your life?

Guided Prayer

Father, Your intention is for all Christian people to realize our union in Christ Jesus. Open our hearts to Your Holy Spirit, promoting what is good, true, and beautiful in each and every one of us. Amen.

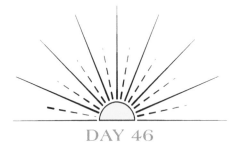

Just Following the Rules

For as we have many members in one body,
but all the members do not have the same function,
so we, being many, are one body in
Christ, and individually members of one another.

—Romans 12:4–5

I have a dear friend who is a mom of many, and as such there are certain guidelines in her house that are nonnegotiable. Some of them are practical, like "Is that a tool or a toy?" or "Sit in a seat that someone is not sitting in." Many are humorous, such as "Don't take your pants off without a plan," or "Tyranny will not be tolerated." But my favorite of the list is "Don't rush off to do a job I gave to someone else." Sure, this family guideline is intended to keep kids from fighting over chores that seem more fun than others (say, washing the car versus cleaning the toilets), but it's a great reminder that God gives each of us a job to do and we should not cast off our own mission in favor of another that seems more desirable.

It's so easy to look at someone else's mission and decide that theirs is better. We begin to compare ourselves to the social media influencer with hundreds of thousands of subscribers (and yes, I fully believe that God does use social media to share His love) and wonder why our mission seems so dull compared to theirs. However, God has given each of us different jobs and different mission fields for a reason. If you have the spiritual gift of teaching, teach. If you have the gift of leadership, start a small group. If you have the gift of hospitality, be the host with the most and share your love of Christ through your space. Your mission field might be a huge college campus or it might just be the people within the walls of your dwelling space. Either way, God has given you a job. Don't rush off to do someone else's.

Wade in the Water

- Why might comparing spiritual gifts lead to jealousy among Christians?

- How can you better come to understand and appreciate your mission?

Daily Action

Whatever gift and mission you have been given, always approach your day with a humble heart, keeping in mind that it's not about what *you* are doing, but what God is doing through you. In your journal, write down your gifts and how you use them for God's glory.

Guided Prayer

Lord, may I accept the job that You've given me with joy and humility rather than with comparison and jealousy. In Christ's name, Amen.

Love Them Anyway

And above all things have fervent love for one another,
for "love will cover a multitude of sins."

—*1 Peter 4:8*

In 1968, at the age of 19, a sophomore at Harvard University, Kent M. Keith, wrote a set of "Paradoxical Commandments" for a student leadership book. While most of us have never heard of Dr. Keith, many of us are familiar with his Paradoxical Commandments because of the work of a small Albanian nun who served the poorest of the poor in Calcutta, India.

Mother Teresa of Calcutta kept a copy of Dr. Keith's commandments posted on the wall of her children's home. The commandments were included in a book about Mother Teresa and because of that, the composition of the commandments have been mistakenly attributed to her. The commandments have undergone a few artistic changes throughout the years, and the modified version has come to be known as the "Anyway" poem; however, the spirit of the commandments remains the same. In short, challenges will come your way, but you should persevere anyway. One of my favorites is the first one: "People are illogical, unreasonable, and self-centered. Love them anyway."

Loving people is difficult, and while we have the free will to set our own values and priorities, the Bible is pretty clear that love should be at the top of the list. Why did God create us? Because He loves us. Why did Jesus die for us? Because He loves us. Why has the Spirit come to dwell among us? Because He loves us. We find meaning and purpose when we love, no matter how challenging, unkind, or, frankly, unlovable the person is. While it's true that when we share our hearts with one another that we open ourselves up to be hurt, we also open ourselves up for love. Protecting our hearts from hurt can also mean missing out on love and sharing love. Christ's hands are our hands. Christ's feet are our feet. Christ's heart dwells within each of us. Love makes a difference.

Wade in the Water

- What are some ways you can show others that you value them as much as God values them?

- What are the consequences of keeping your heart protected from hurt?

Daily Action

Find a copy of the "Anyway" poem and write it out. Paste it to a board and see if you can name someone or a circumstance in your life that matches with each of the directives.

Guided Prayer

Lord Jesus, I can proclaim that I am Christian all day, but if I do not have love, I am "a clanging cymbal" (1 Corinthians 13:1). Grant me the grace to remember that love comes first and the rest is all details. Amen.

Justice, Mercy, Humility

*He has shown you, O man, what is good; and what
does the Lord require of you but to do justly,
to love mercy, and to walk humbly with your God?*

—*Micah 6:8*

As Christians, it can be really easy to get caught up in legalism, just like the people of Israel did when the prophet Micah was speaking. In a sense, legalism is when we feel that we can please God or get into His good graces by making sure we follow all the rules to a T. For Christians, that could seem fairly simple; after all, Jesus distilled 613 mitzvot (Jewish laws or commandments) down to really only two commandments and created a new covenant for God's people, surpassing the old Abrahamic covenant. And yet we can still get caught up in a legalistic mindset. It's easy to let our minds take over when our hearts should be leading. We think to ourselves, *As long as I do everything "right," God will keep on loving me.* But guess what? We will never do everything right, and God will always love us.

This is the concept at the heart of the verse from Micah. God does not require animal sacrifice or elaborate rituals or no mistakes. If we truly want God's will to be done here on earth as it is in heaven, we are called to be fair, merciful, and humble. We ensure these things through our faith because we know it's not just about us; we serve someone more powerful. On the surface, this seems like it should be pretty simple to live out, but this challenge from God, as described by the prophet Micah, stretches our hearts and minds. It is through stepping out with God and trusting His Spirit that we can truly see His kingdom come.

Wade in the Water

- Think of a time when you withheld mercy from someone. What happened? What made granting mercy difficult?

- Why do you think God puts such emphasis on justice, mercy, and humility?

Daily Action

Focus today on having a heart of kindness. Do a random act of kindness for someone. You might let someone go ahead of you in line, pay the bill for the car behind you in the drive-through, or leave a note to compliment someone's amazing parking job. Be creative!

Guided Prayer

Father God, thank You for allowing us to go through life together and giving us the ability to do our little part to make Your kingdom come here on earth. Amen.

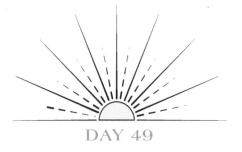

Rolling Like a River

Take away from Me the noise of your songs, for I will not hear the melody of your stringed instruments. But let justice run down like water, and righteousness like a mighty stream.

—*Amos 5:23–24*

After the death of King Solomon, the Kingdom of Israel split into two kingdoms: the Northern Kingdom (also called the Kingdom of Israel and the Kingdom of Samaria) and the Southern Kingdom (the Kingdom of Judah). Amos was a prophet from the Southern Kingdom who was tasked with telling the Northern Kingdom that God was not at all happy with them and their choices. Today, we may see the word *prophet* and picture someone who is able to gaze into a crystal ball to see the future, but the job of a biblical prophet was more like that person we all know who will tell you the truth, no matter how much it hurts to hear. Amos was sent by God to the Northern Kingdom to tell people that they were missing the message.

The Northern Kingdom had wealth and prosperity and enjoyed worshiping God with big festivals, rituals, and elaborate sacrifices. However, economic injustice and disparity was running rampant in the kingdom. The wealthy were very wealthy, and the poor were very poor. If this is beginning to hit a little too close to home, there is a reason for it.

Given the choice, God would much rather prefer that we tend to those most in need around us rather than throw a festival in His honor. It is not so much *what* we are doing, but *who* we are serving. We see time and time again a call for justice, not where each person gets punished for wrongdoing, but where we cultivate genuine relationships with one another and with God. It's the idea that we are right and just when our hearts and actions are aligned with that of God.

Wade in the Water

- Often social justice discussions involve the "what." How would the outcome of the discussions change if we focused on the "who"?

- Why would God make caring for the neediest among us so important?

Daily Action

What does "social justice" mean to you? Take out your journal and describe what it is and how you can live out God's vision for that justice.

Guided Prayer

Lord in heaven, forgive me for the times my personal politics and ideologies blind me to Your Divine will. Through Christ, Amen.

It Is Well with My Soul

He uncovers deep things out of darkness, and brings the shadow of death to light.

—*Job 12:22*

E ven if you are not overly familiar with the Bible, you may be familiar with the story of Job. Job is a man who seems to have it all: property, a great family, and a reputation for being blameless and upright. This leads to a discussion between God and Satan. Satan says that Job is only a good person because God has blessed Him so abundantly, and if he were stripped of everything he had, Job would turn away from God. Satan then asks if he can spend some time tormenting Job to prove to God that Job will turn from Him, and God allows it, provided that Satan does *not* take Job's life. Instead, Satan takes everything else from him (his children, his livestock, even his health), but Job refuses to curse God.

In the 19th century, Horatio G. Spafford was a player in his own Job story. A prominent lawyer and minister, Mr. Spafford had it all until tragedy struck, leaving him and his wife in the shadow of death. In 1873, his wife and four daughters were headed across the Atlantic Ocean on a planned trip to Europe when the ship was struck by another sailing vessel, killing 226 people, including all four of Spafford's daughters. Mr. Spafford was informed of the tragedy by a telegram from his wife, who was recovering in England, which read, "Saved alone."

Out of this story of tragedy came a hymn that has helped me through many personal struggles and tragedies, including an extended hospital stay for our youngest child. "It Is Well with My Soul" describes continued trust in God even when the world is at its darkest. To read the hymn, see the References on page 186.

Wade in the Water

- How do you continue to trust in God, especially when life is challenging?

- Do you think it is easier or more difficult to give to God when you have lots of earthly treasures? Why or why not?

Daily Action

Preparing for adversity requires a healthy mindset. Spend today developing a plan that would help you move forward when hard times come, making sure you are ready for an emergency or natural disaster. You might have a practical plan of what to do in an emergency or a spiritual plan for when you are feeling spiritually overwhelmed because of an emergency. Be prepared!

Guided Prayer

Father, it is easy for me to be a good steward of all You have given to me when life is good. Guide me to trust in You and do Your will even when life is not going my way. In Christ's name, Amen.

The Golden Rule

*Therefore, whatever you want men to do to you,
do also to them, for this is the Law and the Prophets.*

—*Matthew 7:12*

It's a rule so simple that even preschoolers know it. It's one of the first rules of life that we learn, and probably one of the hardest to apply. The Golden Rule states, "Do onto others as you would have them do to you." Oftentimes we use this rule to apply to behavior (e.g., if you don't want your sister to hit you, do not hit your sister), but if we look at this verse from the Gospel according to Matthew, this is less about behavior and more about action. This verse comes from the chapter in which Jesus is instructing His followers about what actions they each should be taking. In this chapter, we are reminded that judgment is best left to God alone, that we should tend to our personal shortcomings before we point out the shortcomings of others, and that we should keep asking, keep seeking, and keep knocking, as our Father in heaven wants nothing more than for us to come to Him with our wants and needs.

Jesus reminds us that our faith is not just about our vertical relationship with God; it is also about our horizontal relationships with one another. Other people *do* matter to us. Other people's sufferings are our sufferings; their joys are our joys. Christianity is not just about me and God. It's about me, God, and everyone else around me. That is why we worship in communion. That is why we join in fellowship. That is why we celebrate, mourn, and support together. In telling us, "Whatever you want men to do to you, do also to them," Jesus reminds us that our faith is not just about what we want and that what we do to and for other people really does matter.

Wade in the Water

- What does this verse tell us about the importance of our actions?

- Was there a time you were the recipient of the Golden Rule? What did that feel like?

Daily Action

Focus on practicing empathy today. Imagine yourself in the shoes of another person and ask how you would like someone else to interact with you. Strive to really understand who they are and what they are going through.

Guided Prayer

Lord Jesus, in Your commandment to us, You challenge us to bring out the best in ourselves and in one another. Please give me opportunities today to practice this commandment of love. Amen.

Wrestling with an Angel

So you, by the help of your God, return; observe mercy and justice, and wait on your God continually.

—*Hosea 12:6*

O f the Old Testament patriarchs, Jacob has one of the more, let's say, colorful backgrounds. Born the second son to Isaac, Jacob is not destined for more than taking care of his father in his old age. However, Jacob's mother has more in mind for him, and sadly it involves deceiving both his brother, Esau, and his father, Isaac. Through a bit of trickery and clever moves, Jacob not only walks away with his father's blessing for the firstborn, but also the firstborn's birthright. This makes his brother, Esau, mad enough to want to kill Jacob. So Jacob runs away.

Years later, after more deception (Jacob himself is tricked into marrying two sisters), Jacob and Esau are to meet up again, and Jacob is not excited about it. He knows his brother has every right to be angry with him, so rather than facing his brother, he runs away again. This time, however, he ends up in a wrestling match with an angel. Jacob, a man whose life has basically been built on deception—wrestling, figuratively, with the will of God—is now literally wrestling with a messenger of God. In sending the angel to wrestle with Jacob, God is asking Jacob if he is willing to accept His help and Divine will, to reconcile with God and become the just and merciful man that God is calling him to be.

Through the story of Jacob, we see how much we rely on God to make us who we are called to be. Jacob eventually overcomes the angel, but only after submitting to God's will for his life. It is when we finally relent and let God lead us that we are able to become the just and merciful people that God calls us to be.

Wade in the Water

- In what areas of your life are you currently wrestling with God?

- Why would God allow Jacob to be deceptive for so much of his life?

Daily Action

Waiting on God is never fun, but the Lord gives us chances to practice waiting every day. Today, when you find yourself waiting, whether for a parking spot or for a coworker to finish a long-winded story, wait with patience, being fully present in the waiting.

Guided Prayer

Father God, open my heart to the areas of my life that I cling to tightly and that I am not willing to give to You. Give me the courage to allow Your will to be done. Amen.

Under the Sun

*For I know the thoughts that I think
toward you, says the Lord, thoughts of peace and not
of evil, to give you a future and a hope.*

—*Jeremiah 29:11*

"It's just not fair!" The lament came from my mouth before I had the chance to stuff it down. It was my senior year of high school and I had just found out that I had been cut from the dance team and that the girl I had spent the summer with helping learn the tryout routines had made the team instead. In my head, she had taken my place. This was my senior year. Who had ever heard of a senior being cut from the team in favor of a freshman? Yet no number of tears or compromises would make the coach change her mind. She was in, and I was out.

Life is not fair. It is full of injustice and wickedness. Most of us will have at least one experience of not getting what we think we deserve. God uses these experiences in our lives to test and teach us. How do we react when life does not go the way we want it to go? Do we turn to God, or do we turn away? Not making the dance team my senior year meant that I had the time to take more AP classes and develop my speaking and writing skills, both of which helped me earn a full scholarship to my state university. Looking back, that temporary pain was a lesson in how we are always called to help and serve one another, even when it means sacrificing something we love to someone else. It also taught me that God's plan is always better than my own.

Wade in the Water

- What might you hope to gain by helping out another person?

- When has God's plan gone against your desires but worked out better in the end?

Daily Action

Be mindful of your reactions today. How do you respond when God's plan goes contrary to what you think His plan should be? When things do not go your way, commit to taking deep breaths and remaining in control and focused on what is above.

Guided Prayer

Father, help me to humble myself to Your will in my life and Your plan for my life, especially when I think that I know better than You.

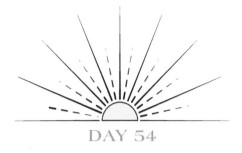

Lead Me, Lord

*And the Lord, He is the One who goes before you.
He will be with you, He will not leave
you nor forsake you; do not fear nor be dismayed.*

—*Deuteronomy 31:8*

When Moses is 120 years old, knowing that his time on earth is coming to an end, he speaks these words to Joshua, his chosen successor to lead the people of Israel. Because of his previous actions, Moses knows he will not be able to enter into the Promised Land of Canaan with the Israelites, so he gives Joshua his blessing to lead them on.

Joshua, feeling the weight of his newfound leadership, is likely filled with a bit of fear and trepidation. Who is he to lead the Israelites? God hasn't spoken to him through a burning bush, so why him? Moses assures Joshua that leadership is not solely dependent on him as a person. Joshua's leadership, like that of Moses, will come from God; God will go before Joshua. God will be with Joshua and will never forsake him. As promised, God is with Joshua as they cross the Jordan River. God stays with him when the walls of Jericho come tumbling down. God does not leave his side as Palestine is conquered by the Israelites.

Each of us is called to lead in our own way. Some of us lead armies, some lead kindergarteners, some lead huge companies, and some lead small teams. Leadership can take on different forms and functions. No two leaders will look or lead the same way. However, your leadership is most effective when you allow God to walk before you. Offer your day to Him in the morning. Ask for His guidance in difficult tasks. And remember, no matter who you are called to lead or how you are called to do it, God goes before you and will never forsake you when you're following His plan.

Wade in the Water

- What qualities of leadership are unique to you and how have they served you?

- Who have you been called to lead? How can you further develop your personal leadership?

Daily Action

What is your next leadership goal? Create a vision board outlining not only your goal but the path you will take to get there. Is there space for Jesus on your board?

Guided Prayer

Father God, just like You promised to never forsake Joshua, I know that You will never forsake me. Be with me today in my thoughts and actions, and help me keep my eyes always fixed on You. Amen.

I Will Rejoice in the Lord

Though the fig tree may not blossom . . .
and there be no herd in the stalls—Yet I will rejoice in
the Lord, I will joy in the God of my salvation.

—Habakkuk 3:17–18

A few summers ago, our family decided to plant a garden. I checked out books on urban gardening from the library, and we researched what fruits and vegetables would grow best in our area. We picked the best spot in our yard, bought the recommended soil, installed an irrigation system, planted our seeds, and settled in to wait. The weeks went by, and our little seedlings grew bigger. Then the blossoms appeared, and we found ourselves daydreaming about the delicious fruits and vegetables that would be on our table in a few weeks. We rejoiced over the tiny baby fruits as they started to develop, knowing that it was just a matter of time. But that time never came. I am not sure what happened, but our baby fruits just stopped growing and died on the vine. For us, this was just an inconvenience. But for Habakkuk and his fellow farmers, a failed harvest could mean poverty or death.

It's easy for us to praise God when things are going well; however, this verse from the book of Habakkuk reminds us that we should also praise God when things are *not* going so well in our lives. Our joy as Christians doesn't come from our circumstances or our environment. Our joy is a decision that we make for ourselves, choosing to remain optimistic in the knowledge that everything will be okay, no matter how bleak things appear. Our joy is saying, "I will rejoice in the Lord!"

Wade in the Water

- Describe a time when you fully trusted God with a great need in your life.

- The trials Habakkuk describes are applicable for an agrarian society. What would the trials look like in an urban or suburban environment?

Daily Action

The book of Habakkuk is perfect for reframing our reactions to trials and tribulations in our lives. Cozy up today with Habakkuk and be open to the message that God has for you.

Guided Prayer

God, You are always present with me, and that alone is reason for rejoicing in You. Help me draw closer to You and make the choice to be joyful in all circumstances. In Christ's name, Amen.

I Just Need to Lie Down

*Then as he lay and slept under a broom tree, suddenly
an angel touched him, and said to him,
"Arise and eat." Then he looked, and there by his head
was a cake baked on coals, and a jar of
water. So he ate and drank, and lay down again.*

—*1 Kings 19:5–6*

God is very much pro-nap. We as productive people tend to be a little anti-nap. Whether it's a feeling of FOMO (fear of missing out) or the fear of not checking off everything on our list, the last thing we want to do is to lie down, no matter how much we need to. The other day, I announced to my four-year-old that it was time for her nap, and she began listing all the reasons why she didn't *need* to take a nap.

As I listened to her attempts at bargaining and justifying why she should be able to skip her nap, I was reminded of the similar reasons I give to myself when I know I just need to go lie down for a little while, like "I don't have the time," "A little more coffee should do it," or "I can sleep in on Saturday."

Rest is a gift from heaven, and it is for all to use. In today's verse, the prophet Elijah is exhausted after several days of intense service to God and having to abruptly flee after a threat was made on his life. Elijah knows that he should probably keep moving, but instead he lies down under a broom tree to take a nap. An angel wakes him up from his nap, gives him a snack and a drink of water, and tells him to take another nap!

We can't do what we are called to do when we are not well rested. Rather than looking at naps as being something for only babies and retired folks, embrace rest to make you the best version of yourself. Sometimes we all just need to lie down.

Wade in the Water

- What are some ways that you refresh yourself? Record them in your journal to remind yourself what you can do when you are feeling overwhelmed.

- How do you justify not slowing down or relaxing when you need rest? Share those justifications with a friend or loved one and reflect on whether or not they ring true.

Daily Action

Take a look at the refresh list you made in your journal. Write down your top three ways to refresh on sticky notes and put them where you won't miss them. They could be physical (drink a glass of water or do 10 jumping jacks), mental (sit down with a crossword puzzle or day-dream for five minutes), or spiritual (offer a prayer of thanksgiving). When it's time for a refresh, choose one and emerge renewed.

Guided Prayer

Father God, grant me the grace to be kind to myself and accept Your invitation of rest when I most need it, especially when I don't think I need it. Through Christ, Amen.

Nothing Is Really Ordinary

*Because He has inclined His ear to me, therefore
I will call upon Him as long as I live . . . I will walk
before the Lord in the land of the living.*

—Psalm 116:2, 9

When my children were younger, we had a time of day that we called The Witching Hour (TWH). It was usually the hour (or two) right before the evening meal when life just fell apart. I would be trying to prepare the meal with a howling toddler at my feet and a baby strapped to my chest. My husband would be on the way home and, since we were living in Los Angeles, inevitably delayed because he was stuck in traffic. One day, when I was lamenting about TWH with a group of friends, one friend shared her personal mantra, which I have since adopted, especially when things are just not going well [emphasis mine]: "I *will walk* before the Lord in the land of the living."

God is not someone we meet after we die; God is right here among us every day of our lives in the ordinary, the mundane, the exciting, and the sad. Yes, God is present in that breathtaking sunset, and He is also present when I am scrubbing the toilet or trying to help one of my children work through some big feelings. God is in everything because God is *of* everything, and everything is precious in His sight.

St. Josemaría Escrívá was a Spanish priest who preached this ordinary and universal call to holiness, the idea that we are invited to meet with God in the everyday actions of our lives. He's quoted as saying, "Your ordinary contact with God takes place where your fellow men, your yearnings, your work and your affections are. There you have your daily encounter with Christ."

Wade in the Water

- How does your outlook of ordinary life change when you choose to see God in the ordinary?

- When you are walking with God, what fears or anxieties disappear?

Daily Action

Read Psalm 116:9 to yourself. Take out your colored pencils, watercolors, crayons, or whatever you have access to and meditate while you create, asking God to reveal new truths to you through His Word and your creativity.

Guided Prayer

Lord, I walk with confidence when I walk with you. Please help me see the beauty in all things, even the ordinary and mundane, as they all are a part of You. Amen.

The Good Physician

They said to His disciples, "Why does your Teacher eat
with tax collectors and sinners?" When
Jesus heard that, He said to them, "Those who are well
have no need of a physician, but those who are sick."

—*Matthew 9:11–12*

The Bible is filled with God using flawed people—or just people whom society decides are not worthy—for His glory. Moses was a murderer, Jonah was vengeful, Naomi was a widow, John and James were so impulsive that Jesus gave them the nickname "Sons of Thunder." Then there was Matthew.

Matthew is a tax collector, which means that he is completely despised by his fellow countrymen. The job of the tax collector was to collect taxes from the people and submit those taxes to Caesar, and many tax collectors had the reputation of inflating the taxes owed and pocketing the difference. So here is Matthew, minding his own business, counting up his coins, when Jesus walks by. Jesus stops, points at Matthew, and simply says, "Follow me." No preamble, no explanation. Matthew follows him; from now on, he is only going to serve God. He drops his coins and is converted. Not only that, but also Jesus and his disciples head back to Matthew's house for a party! The Pharisees, who are the pious religious leaders of the day, see Jesus hanging out with Matthew and other tax collectors and various sinners in the area and are appalled at His actions. Jesus simply points out to them that "those who are well have no need of a physician, but those who are sick."

Jesus is not impressed by those who seem sinless or pretend they are sinless; rather, He comes for those who know they are flawed and *still* come to Him. He comes for those who are willing to look outside themselves toward something better. Jesus can do so much with each and every one of us, no matter how imperfect we may be. We just have to be willing to stand up and follow Him.

Wade in the Water

- How does withholding compassion and mercy from one another make us no better than the Pharisees?

- In what ways can self-righteousness keep us away from God?

Daily Action

Walking as a disciple means giving up on things that we love but might not be good for us. Are there habits or things in your life that you just can't fully give up? Write one down on a slip of paper and throw it away (or recycle it!), giving it over to God.

Guided Prayer

Jesus, You called those burdened by sin and cast aside by society to come and follow You. May I never forget that I am always in need of a good physician. Amen.

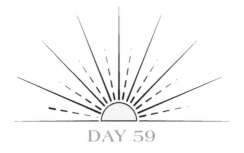

Let Your Yes Mean Yes

*Therefore, when I was planning this,
did I do it lightly? Or the things I plan, do I plan
according to the flesh, that with me there
should be Yes, Yes, and No, No? But as God is faithful,
our word to you was not Yes and No.*

—*2 Corinthians 1:17–18*

The Corinthians were mad at Paul. In a previous letter to the church at Corinth, Paul promised to come and visit them in person. Life happened, and because Paul was not able to keep his promise to the Corinthians, he sent a letter explaining the change in plans. While Paul felt pretty good about this solution, some members of the church were not happy. Paul was accused of being untrustworthy, someone who goes against his word. His integrity was broken with the Corinthians, and they made sure that he knew it.

Integrity is something that you don't notice when it is intact, but you can 100 percent see when it is broken. Integrity is letting your yesses mean yes and your nos mean no. For me, broken integrity manifests in physical stress—my muscles get tense, I get an uneasy feeling in my gut, and I clench my jaw, and these symptoms remain until my integrity has been restored. When we are in integrity, we are integrated, we are intact, we are whole with everything around us. When our integrity with someone breaks (because it can and does happen), the first thing that we have to do is to acknowledge that brokenness. If I made an agreement to meet someone at 5:00 p.m. and I show up 30 minutes later, no matter the reason, my integrity has been broken. Acknowledging broken integrity not only brings the issue into light, it also allows for reconciliation and reconnection.

Wade in the Water

- What does integrity mean to you?

- How can you avoid breaking your integrity with others? Maybe it's looking at your calendar to make sure you really do have the time or putting away your phone to give someone your full attention.

Daily Action

Oftentimes we agree to things to make others happy. Make sure that your yes really means yes today by not committing to anything until you have some time to think about it and respond mindfully.

Guided Prayer

Father in heaven, I am a person of integrity who knows that my integrity will be broken. Please give me the courage to acknowledge my broken integrity and seek reconciliation with those I have hurt. Amen.

Disciples Are Decision-Makers

Jesus, looking at him, loved him, and said . . .
"One thing you lack: Go your way, sell whatever you
have and give to the poor, and you will have
treasure in heaven; and come, take up the cross, and
follow Me." But he . . . went away sorrowful,
for he had great possessions.

—Mark 10:21–22

Wouldn't it be nice if we all had a Moses moment when making choices? You know the feeling when you are wrestling with a big decision or trying to figure out what God wants from you, and you have no idea what to do? Wouldn't it be great to hear the voice of God whisper in your ear the answer that you are seeking? Why can't God just tell us what we should do? Alas, we are called to be decision-makers. That's right, disciples are decision-makers.

Think about when Jesus calls the 12 disciples. He gives each of them a choice: remain where they are or follow Him. He does not make the decision for them; they have to make the choice. Today's verse talks about the rich young man who has the chance to be a disciple and chooses otherwise. God already knows what we want and need, but we still have to make the decisions because of the gift of free will. God could have easily made us mindless robots who would obey His every command, or He could have been a vengeful, tyrannical God forcing our actions. Thankfully, neither of those are true. He is a loving God who wants us to choose Him on our own.

Each of us is called to decide all over again every morning: Will I serve, or will I not serve? Will I choose to follow or choose to walk away? We are the only ones who can make those decisions for ourselves. Let our decisions be made out of love for God, not fear.

Wade in the Water

- Why do you think Jesus tells the man to sell everything?

- What has been the hardest decision for you to make in the last month? What made it so hard?

Daily Action

It's easy to see this teaching as being only about wealth, but it's bigger than that. It's about having a change of heart. Create a timeline, beginning when you first decided to follow Christ, making a note of the times when you had to choose to turn toward Christ and away from something in the world. Make note of the outcomes of those decisions on your timeline.

Guided Prayer

Lord Jesus, every morning, let me wake up and choose to follow You. Thank You for the gift of free will and may I always choose to serve. Amen.

Leaving the Ninety-Nine

"What do you think? If a man has a hundred sheep, and one of them goes astray, does he not leave the ninety-nine and go to the mountains to seek the one that is straying?

—Matthew 18:12

W e had just pulled into the driveway of our new house after a three-day trip across the country. We were so excited to not have to sleep in a hotel room and even more excited to not have to spend hours in the van. We all piled out and started exploring our new spaces. After a few minutes, I looked around and asked my husband, "Where's Edith?" We all started poking around inside, looking in closets and in bedrooms, but no Edith. Slowly the anxiety started creeping in, as our four-year-old was nowhere to be found.

Fanning out, we all searched the property and started calling her name. It was one of our older children who heard her small voice shouting back, "What?" upon hearing our shouts. There she was, two doors down, playing with some backyard toys. As we reunited, our heartbeats slowing, I was reminded how much Jesus rejoices when we are reunited with Him.

Sheep were a common and valuable part of life for the ancient Hebrews and other nomadic people of the desert lands. Sheep could provide a family with food, milk, and clothing and were used in ritual sacrifice. It should be no surprise that a shepherd would go to great lengths to not only protect his flock but seek out those who became lost. A single sheep, separated from the flock, is helpless and liable to fall victim to predators or the surrounding environment. A good shepherd would not hesitate to leave his flock to locate one lost sheep and ensure their safe return. As we could not rest until we had found our Edith, Jesus does not hesitate to seek out each of us when we go astray, carrying us back to the flock in His loving arms.

Wade in the Water

- Can you remember a time when you lost something valuable? What did that feel like?

- How does the parable of the lost sheep show the importance of each of us to God?

Daily Action

Make an effort to reach out to someone who seems separated from Christ. Maybe that means inviting them to attend a church service with you or just showing them love, compassion, and hospitality.

Guided Prayer

Dear Jesus, thank You for being a good shepherd, seeking us when we go astray, and singing over us when we are found. Amen.

A Mother's Love

I do not know how your life began in my womb,
she would say, I was not the one who gave you life and
breath and put together each part of your body.
It was God who did it, God who created the universe,
the human race, and all that exists. He is merciful
and he will give you back life and breath again,
because you love his laws more than you love yourself.

—*2 Maccabees 7:22–23 (GNT)*

On December 7, 1988, an earthquake struck Armenia at 11:41 a.m. Children were in school, people were at work, and a mother and daughter were visiting a family member when the building around them began to tremble and sway. When it was all over, the mother and daughter had fallen five stories to the basement of the apartment building, where they were trapped by tons of concrete and prefabricated walls, entombed in perpetual night with only a jar of jam to sustain them.

Most of us have heard the survival rule of threes: You can survive three minutes in icy water, three hours in a harsh environment, three days without water, and three weeks without food. The mother and daughter were fortunate enough to have air to breathe and a jar of jam to eat, and the environment around them was fairly stable, albeit a bit cold—but water was going to be a problem. So, the mother did something drastic, something that very well may have saved her daughter. For eight days, she sacrificed of herself, cutting her fingers open, sustaining her daughter with her blood. They both survived.

The love of a parent is powerful. The love of our Father God can get us through life's most difficult challenges. In today's verse, the Maccabean mother has seen her seven sons martyred for refusing to break God's commandments, and she has steadfastly refused to submit herself to the whims of the king. She recognizes that man's earthly power is no match for God's, and she bears her grief and hardship bravely because of her trust in the Lord. While we don't know the outcome of every situation, we do know that faith leads to hope, hope leads to love, and God's love never fails.

Wade in the Water

- What would you be most willing to sacrifice for another?

- If the Armenian mother had been alone, do you think she would have survived or given up? Why?

Daily Action

Sacrifice something of comfort today—cream in your coffee, a hot shower, or a comfy pillow—to unite yourself with those who are hopeful in the midst of suffering.

Guided Prayer

Father, when my love fails, let me fall back on hope. When hope fails, let me fall back on faith. Strengthen my faith to remember that You will never leave me. Amen.

Truth Be Told

Woe to you, scribes and Pharisees, hypocrites! For you cleanse the outside of the cup and dish, but inside they are full of extortion and self-indulgence. Blind Pharisee, first cleanse the inside of the cup and dish, that the outside of them may be clean also.

—Matthew 23:25–26

How are you?

It's a rhetorical question that we ask and answer countless times during the day in a way that may or may not be 100 percent truthful. After all, most of us respond with a reflexive "I am well!" or "I'm fine," and then we move on to the rest of the conversation without really getting into how we are *actually* doing or *really* feeling. We are good at hiding what we would prefer the world not see, but what if we really let our outside match what we were feeling inside?

The Pharisees were really good at this sort of thing, making sure they appeared to have it all together as seemingly perfect examples of what Jewish citizens should be. They were fastidious about following all the rules and notorious for calling out those who appeared to be breaking them. On the outside, they were pious and God-fearing, but Jesus, who could see straight into their souls, saw them for what they really were: self-indulgent, full of extortion, and sinful.

As Christian singer Matthew West suggests in his song "Truth Be Told," we tend to have an idea of what the perfect Christian looks, sounds, and acts like—but our idea is false. There is no perfect Christian. We all fail, and we all fall short of the glory that God designed us for. That's why we need Jesus. Let's work to make our outsides match our insides by cleaning out what is inside. Let's let the truth be told.

Wade in the Water

- Why is it easier for us to play a part than to be real?

- Who do you feel most similar to: The Pharisees? The people listening? Jesus? Why?

Daily Action

Choose today to be fully honest and real. If you are not doing well, share that fact. If things are amazing, shout it from the rooftops. Always remember that being truthful with yourself and others, when done in love, is something to strive for.

Guided Prayer

Father in heaven, create in me a clean heart, O Lord (Psalm 51), and allow Your character to shine through me, both internally and externally. Through Christ, Amen.

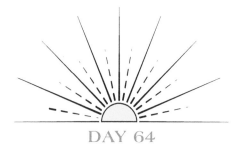

Never a Bad Time

Cause me to hear Your lovingkindness in the morning,
for in You do I trust; cause me to know the way
in which I should walk, for I lift up my soul to You.

—*Psalm 143:8*

I am a morning person, and I have been one for as long as I can remember. In college, I was more than happy to sign up for that 8:00 a.m. class, and the 5:00 a.m. shift at work was my jam. Dawn is when I feel most connected to God, and it is the time when I prefer to spend time in prayer and in God's Word.

Life changed after college: I got married, we had children, and things were no longer about me and my preferences. Late nights would blend into early mornings, and I was snatching time wherever I could just to speak more than three words to God. I found myself drifting further and further away because I was not willing to try to really sit with God where I was, instead focusing on how God just didn't fit into my life anymore. Thankfully, our God is patient. He is always there for us, waiting for us to return to Him. I shed my rigid thinking and started meeting God in my everyday tasks. Meeting God was not about sitting for an hour with His Word; it was about seeing prayers that I posted around the house, singing songs of praise with the radio, and serving my family and others with joy.

But as the book of Ecclesiastes reminds us, nothing ever remains the same. My kids are older and no longer wake up as soon as they hear me puttering about. I have time now to sit in the silence of the dawn and let God's lovingkindness wash over me. However, I still have those prayers posted around my house and life-giving music on the radio at all times, and I still try to serve those around me with love, affection, and joy.

Wade in the Water

- When things in life seem overwhelming, how do you remember to reach for God?

- What are some ways to make sure your prayer is heartfelt rather than an automatic response?

Daily Action

In your journal, list the ways you have trusted God and how His promises have been fulfilled to you. What are your God moments and miracles in life?

Guided Prayer

Father, guide me in the paths that You have carved out for me, which will allow me to continue the work that Your Son began here on earth. In Jesus's name, Amen.

Talitha, Cumi

Then He took the child by the hand,
and said to her, "Talitha, cumi," which is translated,
"Little girl, I say to you, arise."

—*Mark 5:41*

The little girl is dead. Her father, Jairus, kneels by her bedside with tears of sorrow and anger rolling down his cheeks. They had said that the teacher was a miracle man. They had said that if you called upon Him, He would come. The girl's father had sent his servant to get Jesus to heal his daughter, but He hadn't come—and now she lies dead. All around are the sounds of weeping and mourning for the child, a child with so much potential, here for 12 years and now gone. The teacher doesn't come.

A commotion outside makes the father raise his head; through teary eyes, he sees a silhouette at the door. He hears someone say that his daughter only sleeps, but those who sleep breathe and there is no breath in this little one. The murmuring voices fade until only the father, the mother, two disciples, and Jesus remain. The father feels the presence of the teacher beside him, but he can't make himself look into the eyes of the one who hasn't come in time. He watches as the teacher takes his daughter by the hand and commands her to arise. Fighting doubt and despair, the father allows a little bubble of hope to settle in his chest, a bubble that grows as he sees his daughter move her fingers and toes. The bubble bursts with joy as she opens her eyes.

Faith, in the midst of despair, is not easy to hold on to, and it's even harder to maintain when we don't have a miracle moment like Jairus and his family had. However, we know that we belong to a God who keeps His promises. When it looks like things are over and done, let Jesus remind us all that He is God incarnate.

Wade in the Water

- How does fear affect your faith?

- How has Jesus brought healing into your life?

Daily Action

In a notebook or journal, create two columns. Title the first column "My requests" and the second column "God's answers." Think back and write about five times you have made requests to God and what His answers were. Which of those requests led to rejoicing?

Guided Prayer

My Lord, You are a God who keeps His promises and stays by our sides, even when things are rough. Thank You for always answering my requests, even when the answer is "No" or "Not now." Through Christ's name, Amen.

On a Mission

*Jesus, walking by the Sea of Galilee, saw two
brothers, Simon called Peter, and Andrew his brother,
casting a net into the sea; for they were fishermen.
Then He said to them, "Follow Me, and I
will make you fishers of men." They immediately left
their nets and followed Him.*

—Matthew 4:18–20

Jesus is a man on a mission, and if you are not fully convinced of that, just open any of the Gospels and read. His mission to save all of humanity from sin jumps out at us. In His mission, Jesus is not just focusing on those who society deems worthy or the rich or powerful; He seeks out those who have been cast aside and are unwanted. Looking more closely, we can see that Jesus executes His mission without trumpets and fanfare. He starts out small and quietly with the calling of two random fishermen: Simon and Andrew.

Simon and Andrew are not wealthy. Most people in Palestine at that time were poor, but as fishermen, Simon and Andrew have means to make a living in an area that thrives on fish. They are not famous, they are not men of influence, and they have zero followers.

All they have are some nets and fish when they can catch some. For all intents and purposes, these two men seem very unlikely to be the first ones to join Jesus on His mission, and yet they are.

Simon and Andrew are great examples for each of us. When Jesus offers to make them "fishers of men," they do not hem and haw and weigh their options. They turn away from their old methods of doing things and walk with Jesus. Put in another way, they believe and repent. Just like Simon and Andrew, we are called to repent and believe and to join Jesus in His mission. What say you?

Wade in the Water

- What do Simon and Andrew leave behind to follow Jesus?

- How is being a "follower of Jesus" different from being a "Christian"?

Daily Action

As a companion on the mission, you should have a goal. What is your goal as a follower of Christ? What are the steps you need to take to achieve your goal? Grab a large sheet of paper and set one to two HARD (heartfelt, animated, required, difficult) faith goals to accomplish this year and the steps you will take to achieve those goals.

Guided Prayer

Lord Jesus, Your mission for humanity was clear, as was my call to follow You. Please inspire me to live out Your Word fully and be a true disciple of You in all that I say and do. Now and forevermore, Amen.

Repent and Believe

. . . Jesus came to Galilee, preaching the gospel of the kingdom of God, and saying, "The time is fulfilled, and the kingdom of God is at hand. Repent, and believe in the gospel."

—*Mark 1:14–15*

In my faith tradition, the beginning of the liturgical season of Lent is marked by an outward sign of ashes on the forehead. Ashes are used throughout the Bible as a sign of grief or repentance, reinforcing the idea that we come from dust and it is to dust that we return. During Lent, we focus on this idea of repentance, of turning away from the old self and embracing the new self. I love how we return to this model year after year, because none of us will ever repent perfectly.

When we accept the call to follow Jesus, we accept the challenge to "repent and believe." For many of us, the believing part is easy. Even though we cannot physically see God, we see enough evidence of His wonder and beauty around us that we can't help but believe. But what about repentance, a full turning away from who we once were? That is a little tougher. Who we were before we took up the cross of Christ might be very different from who we are now, and that change is not easy—either for us as individuals or for those who knew us before. It's not easy, but sometimes the best things for us are also the hardest.

Repentance is something we have to choose and work on every single day. Each morning when you wake up, when you begin your workday, when you meet friends for coffee or a night out, you have a new opportunity to repent and believe. We are invited to emulate Christ in our words and actions and to turn away from habits or actions that do not draw us nearer to Christ. "Repent and believe" is not just a one-time invitation; it is an ongoing process.

Wade in the Water

- How do you know that you have repented?

- What are the hardest things for you to turn away from?

Daily Action

Take out your journal. When we choose to repent and believe, we become a new creation in Christ (2 Corinthians 5:17). Think back on how you have changed from who you were before following Christ. In what ways are you better? In what ways are you worse?

Guided Prayer

Dear Jesus, in a world of unbelievers, please help me not only continue to believe in the good things that You have planned for me but also to repent against who I was before You rescued me. Amen.

Living in the Moment

I am not saying this because I am in need, for I have learned to be content whatever the circumstances. I know what it is to be in need, and I know what it is to have plenty. I have learned the secret of being content in any and every situation . . .

—Philippians 4:11–12, NIV

A few years ago at a family picnic my husband struck up a conversation with another man. They both seemed to hit it off well—they were both fathers of young children, they both worked in the same industry, and they were both acquainted with the same people. They made a plan to have lunch the following week, and my husband walked away with the joyful thought of having made a new friend, which, as we all know, can be really hard when you are an adult!

The day of their lunch rolled around and toward the end of the meal, this gentleman turned to my husband and said, "So, what do you want from me?" My husband was quite taken aback by this statement because, frankly, he did not want anything from this other man other than friendship. Whereas my husband looked at their meeting as a social event, this other gentleman looked at their meeting as a means to an end—strictly utilitarian.

For all the advances our society has made, we sure have become utilitarian. We go to school to get an education to get a job. We run, jump, and lift heavy objects to get in shape. We meet for lunch to get contacts. We are not content to do things just for the joy of doing them. This is what Paul was encouraging the people of Philippi to remember: There is a joy in being content with where you are in life. Rather than looking back with longing at the past or focusing on what is to come, living in the moment and finding the joy in the present reminds us what a beautiful gift life is and how every moment on earth is special and matters.

Wade in the Water:

- How would you describe contentment?

- What was the last thing that you did just for fun?

Daily Action

Today, call up a friend and do something just for fun. Maybe it's going to the park to swing on the swings, strolling through a farmers' market, or finding a crowded spot and people watching. Whatever you choose, put your phone away and live in the moment.

Guided Prayer

Father, please help me avoid a utilitarian mindset and remind me that having fun and living in the moment are all part of Your plan for us. May I always find contentment with what is right in front of me. In Jesus's name, Amen.

Serve All, Save Some

For though I am free from all men,
I have made myself a servant to all, that I might win
the more . . . I have become all things
to all men, that I might by all means save some.

—*1 Corinthians 9:19, 22*

On Day 66, we talked about sharing in Christ's mission here on earth (page 132), which is something we should take seriously. In the Gospel of Matthew, Jesus lays out what that mission is: to go out into the world and make disciples of all nations (Matthew 28:19). So, we know what we are supposed to be doing, but how exactly are we supposed to accomplish this goal? What is the best way to reach out with the Gospel of Jesus?

You might be thinking of tangible things: mission trips overseas, inviting people to church, reaching out to those around us, financially supporting our churches. But once we have exhausted the ideas of outreach and church missions, what is left? In his first letter to the church at Corinth, Paul gives us a pretty good idea: Serve all people to save some. We should reach out to all, not just the some that we like. We should share our personal stories of conversion with the idea that repenting and believing also means leaving behind our old selves. The freedom we have in Christ is the same freedom with which we are called to serve others. We are called to serve and thereby share the love of Christ. We are not called to save, because only Jesus can save. It's not about saving all or saving some or saving one; it is about serving all.

Wade in the Water

- How can you be sure that you are serving others with Christ in mind?

- In what ways are you using your gifts of time, treasure, and talent to serve others?

Daily Action

Make a list of three to five people you would love to share the Gospel with. Decide in what way the message will be best shared. Is it through service, your personal testimony, a frank conversation? Once you have made your plan, go out into the world and share the Good News!

Guided Prayer

Father, we are called to love our neighbor as ourselves and in love. Love does not hide truth from another. Please help me strive to live in your truth, always. In Christ's name, Amen.

Just Like Me

*[He] made Himself of no reputation,
taking the form of a bondservant, and coming in the
likeness of men. And being found in appearance
as a man, He humbled Himself and became obedient to
the point of death, even the death of the cross.*

—*Philippians 2:7–8*

There is the saying that "opposites attract," but a 2016 study published in the *Journal of Personality and Social Psychology* supports the idea that we are more attracted to, and are more trusting of, those who act more like us. Over time, we become more like each other, not because we are subconsciously influencing each other, but because those qualities of like-mindedness were already there.

On a certain level it makes sense. As we know ourselves, we are most comfortable being around people who remind us of ourselves, both for better or for worse. This is exactly what Jesus did. Jesus is the Son of God and could have come to earth in the full glory of God, great and terrible. Instead, he came as a baby born into poor and humble circumstances. He could have ministered from a position of absolute authority, enforcing obedience through fear and coercion. Instead, He was all about the relationship, reaching out to those on the outside of society and teaching with stories. He could have saved all of us with a single word. Instead, He became a man, lived among us, and died a physical death, all to conquer death and give us everlasting life.

Whether it was because He wanted to give us a never-before-seen revelation of God or fulfill the Old Testament prophecies, or because He knew that an actual, physical act of sacrifice would make us finally sit up and listen, Jesus became like one of us so He could meet each one of us.

Wade in the Water

- How are you like your friends? How are you different from your friends?

- In what ways did Jesus take on the qualities of a servant?

Daily Action

How would your faith and your response to Jesus be different if He came as a great and terrible king rather than a vulnerable baby? Would you be more or less willing to share about Jesus? Would He be as approachable? Write a few lines in your journal today with this in mind.

Guided Prayer

Lord Jesus, thank You for being willing to lay down Your life for me. Walk with me today as I strive to better live out Your example of leading by serving others. Amen.

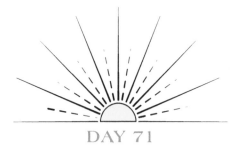

Transformed by Renewal

And do not be conformed to this world,
but be transformed by the renewing of your mind, that
you may prove what is that good and acceptable
and perfect will of God.

—*Romans 12:2*

One of the major milestones in Jesus's life is the mystery of the transfiguration (Matthew 17). In this event, Jesus, along with Peter, James, and John, head to a mountain where something awe-inspiring happens. Jesus's appearance changes before them into a glorified body, with His clothes white and His face shining like the sun. Before their eyes, the full glory of God the Son as the connection between heaven and earth, the eternal and the temporal, is revealed.

We, too, are called to be changed—not transfigured but transformed. While these two words sound the same, they mean very different things. As explained by Bishop Nicholas Knisely on his blog, *Entangled States*, transfiguration involves a revelation of something that was previously hidden in plain sight. To be transfigured means to have a true nature revealed, as Jesus's was. Transformation, on the other hand, is a remaking of one's nature into something that hasn't previously existed. For Christians, transformation means the Holy Spirit changes us, from the outside in and the inside out, into a new creation.

We allow the Holy Spirit to transform us from the outside through studying God's Word, seeking out Christ-centered communities, hearing the Gospel, and reading spiritual writings. We are transformed from the inside when we embrace humility, allow our hardened hearts to be broken, and show love to those different from us. Transformation helps us more fully live out the "good, acceptable, and perfect will of God."

Wade in the Water

- Is it harder to change from the inside or outside? Why?

- What is the good, acceptable, and perfect will of God?

Daily Action

Contemplate how your actions relate to the highs and lows in your life. Are your reactions those of someone conformed to the world or transformed by the Spirit? In your journal, record areas that can be improved. Maybe you are quick to get angry or easily exasperated by others. How can the Spirit help you soften those reactions?

Guided Prayer

Father in heaven, please be with me as I align myself with Your Will. Help me give up the desire to do what I want and commit to what You want for my life. Amen.

Focus Up, Squirrel!

*Let your eyes look straight ahead,
and your eyelids look right before you. Ponder the path
of your feet, and let all your ways be established.*

—*Proverbs 4:25–26*

I have a confession to make: I am very easily distracted by life around me. It used to drive my husband up the wall when he would come across some half-finished project or task around our house. A peanut butter sandwich half-made, a few pieces of laundry folded with the rest in the basket and me off reading a book. His biggest pet peeve? Jars with tops that are only partially screwed on to the point where the top comes off in your hand and the jar crashes to the floor with jelly and glass flying everywhere. Not that that's ever happened.

I can't help it. Even when I am in the middle of accomplishing something, if another thing pops into my head, I have to stop and start that until I get distracted again. My husband affectionately calls me "Squirrel," but there are times when my distractions can be dangerous. Driving on the freeway, cooking at the stove, and walking near traffic all need my full attention. I've had to work at disciplining myself to complete one thing before beginning another.

I've embraced making lists and turning off any and all notifications on my mobile device.

It is not easy to retrain yourself to focus on one thing at a time; however, not only are there fewer half-finished projects around my house now, but I am less anxious and stressed out because I am more fully aware of who I am. When we know who we are in Christ, we are better able to walk the path with our eyes straight ahead.

Wade in the Water

- What are some benefits of focusing on one thing rather than multitasking?

- What are some of the dangers of trying to do too many things at once?

Daily Action

Today, focus on "completing the cycle." If you take something out of your cupboard to use, you are not "done" until the item is back in place. If you begin a task, finish the task before moving on. Slow down while you eat today and be mindful of all the sensations. Put on some music and just sit and listen to it. Be present in everything you do.

Guided Prayer

Father, there are so many wonderful and amazing things around us that we can easily lose focus on what we are doing. With Your grace, grant us the ability to remain focused and to complete the important things first. Amen.

Keeping Our Word

When you make a vow to God, do not delay to pay it;
for He has no pleasure in fools. Pay what you have
vowed—better not to vow than to vow and not pay.

—*Ecclesiastes 5:4–5*

Have you ever tried to make a deal with God? You know the scene: You are deep in prayer with something heavy on your heart and you say to the Lord, "God, if you can just make this one thing happen, I promise never to ask you for anything else!" Or maybe it sounds more like, "Lord, if You help me win the lottery, I will give half of it away!" Or, "Lord, if you will make this traffic disappear, I will do whatever you want."

God is not a genie. We don't get three wishes, and we certainly cannot wish for more wishes. Making rash bargains with the God of the universe is not only insincere, but also it can be dangerous to our souls. We know that lying to other people is a sin, so why wouldn't lying to God also be a sin, even if the lie is not the intention? Besides, those who make deals with God and fail to follow through are classified as "fools" in the Bible. It is foolish to make a deal that we either cannot or will not follow through with, so we need to make sure we are always people of our word. As Jesus reminds us during His Sermon on the Mount, we have to let our yes mean yes and our no mean no and not settle for anything in between.

When you feel yourself about to make a rash vow, take a deep breath and instead pray this line from the Our Father: "Thy will be done." When we focus on following God's will rather than our own desires, we are less likely to make rash bargains or promises we cannot keep.

Wade in the Water

- Why is it so tempting to treat God as a genie whose only purpose is to fulfill our desires?

- How can you make sure that you follow through with your promises?

Daily Action

Throughout your day today, focus on God's will in your life. Before heading to bed tonight, record in your journal any instances from your day when you allowed God's will to be done rather than fighting for your own.

Guided Prayer

Jesus, the words You taught us are simple: "Thy will be done." May I resist the temptation to treat God as a wish-fulfiller and see Him for what He is: a gift-giver. Amen.

His Mercy Endures Forever

Oh, give thanks to the Lord, for He is good . . .
Who remembered us in our lowly state . . .
and rescued us from our enemies . . . Who gives food
to all flesh . . . Oh, give thanks to the
God of heaven! For His mercy endures forever.

—*Psalm 136:1, 23–36*

There is a common thought that seems to penetrate the Christian consciousness: the idea that having a deep connection with, and faith in, the Lord means that you will no longer suffer or feel anger or sadness, that faith in Jesus is a magic salve that makes all negative emotions disappear like the seeds of a dandelion puff in the summer. While this sounds fine and dandy, what happens when, despite your deep faith, you find yourself becoming angry, upset, or just plain sad? Does this mean your faith is not as strong as you thought? Does this mean you don't love Jesus as much as you think you do? No. This means that you are human.

When Jesus arrives after Lazarus's death, Martha and Mary are heartbroken and angry because Jesus hasn't come right away, yet their faith is so strong that they know whatever He speaks into existence will happen. After the crucifixion, when Mary holds the broken body of her son in her arms and cries tears of sorrow, she knows it isn't the end of the story. The Israelites endure numerous trials as they wander for 40 years in the desert, yet they eventually reach the promised land, even if their praise is hard to hear over their grumbling

Feeling unhappy, angry, irritable, or impatient are not signs of a lack of faith, but they can help reinforce our faith, reminding us that God can make good out of anything, as long as we let Him.

Wade in the Water

- What are some ways you can be sure to praise God in all things?

- How do you go about controlling your emotions rather than letting your emotions control you?

Daily Action

In your journal today, pick five times of the day. Something basic like morning, midmorning, noon, afternoon, and bedtime. At each of those times, record your mood at that moment and write down something that is praiseworthy around you. When you are done, make a list to remind yourself of all the good that is around you, even when life is challenging.

Guided Prayer

Father in heaven, thank You for creating me as a living, breathing, thinking, and feeling creature. Help me understand that all feelings have value and none should be discounted or avoided. In Jesus's name, Amen.

Our Souls
Magnify the Lord

And Mary said: "My soul magnifies the Lord, and my spirit has rejoiced in God my Savior."

—*Luke 1:46–47*

These lines are the beginning of a song, known as the "Magnificat," that Mary sings during her visit to her cousin Elizabeth. Mary is rejoicing in her own impossible pregnancy, and they are celebrating Elizabeth's as well, since, as described in Luke 1, Elizabeth is barren, and she and her husband are both advanced in age (Luke 1:7). Here we have two women, chosen by God to do great things in the world, and the first thing that Mary does is give thanks and sing her praises to God. What a great example to us!

Mary opens with a simple statement: "My soul magnifies the Lord." One definition of "magnify" is to intensify, to make something greater. Rather than singing about her pregnancy or how great her actions are, she rejoices that her very soul is being used to intensify the Lord—both literally, in that her body is carrying the Son of God, and figuratively, in that the Lord is being intensified through her "fiat," her "yes."

Mary's "yes" starts a whole series of events that could turn out very badly if not for the blessing of the Lord on her life. Unlike her cousin, Mary is not yet married, and she knows that, according to the social norms of the time, she can be ostracized or even killed if it is discovered that she is carrying a child as an unmarried woman. While some imagine this song as a gentle song of praise, considering the circumstances, I've always seen it as Mary's song of defiance as she looks forward to an unknown future.

Wade in the Water

- Why does Mary choose not to remain silent and hidden about what is happening in her life?

- How do you praise God for His actions in your life?

Daily Action

Compose the beginning of your own "Magnificat." How does your soul magnify the Lord? How does your Spirit rejoice in God?

Guided Prayer

Lord God, allow my soul to magnify You and the goodness that comes from You. May songs of praise be on my lips today, tomorrow, and always. Amen.

From Hannah, with Love

For He has regarded the lowly state of His maidservant; for behold, henceforth all generations will call me blessed. For He who is mighty has done great things for me, and holy is His name.

—Luke 1:48–49

The virgin birth of Jesus and the miraculous birth of John the Baptist are not the first miracle births in the Bible. Sarah laughs when she finds out she is pregnant with Isaac despite being way past her childbearing years, and Hannah sings a song of praise rejoicing in her son, Samuel. Both of these women are great examples of how nothing is impossible with God.

Mary's song, quoted above and in Day 75, bears a striking resemblance to Hannah's song in the Old Testament, which leads us to believe that Mary's faith is likely well-rooted in Jewish tradition. She believes in the one God, the Father almighty, and she knows her scripture so well that she models her own song of praise after Hannah's.

We meet Hannah in the first book of Samuel. Like Sarah before her and Elizabeth many generations later, Hannah is barren and deemed of little worth to society. Hannah also has the additional burden of being one of two wives to her husband, Elkanah. Like Rachel before her, she's had to deal with watching the other wife give birth to child after child, while her womb remains closed. So Hannah does something that the book of Ecclesiastes warns us not to do lightly: She makes a deal with God. If God will give her a son, she will give that son back to God. The prophet Samuel is born to Hannah, and Hannah sings her own song of praise to the Lord. True to her word, when he is old enough, Hannah gives her child in service to God under Eli. Like Hannah, we can sometimes be considered unworthy, but we are always worthy to God, Who will do great things for us.

Wade in the Water

- What is the hardest part about giving something you love to God?

- How do we see human value being placed on things we can't control, like physical characteristics or environmental circumstances?

Daily Action

Take out your Bible, look up Hannah's song (1 Samuel 2:1–10), and compare and contrast Hannah's song with Mary's song in Luke 1:46–55. In your journal, reflect on their similarities and differences.

Guided Prayer

Father God, while Hannah may not have been valued by those around her, she was a precious treasure in Your sight. Please help me see that my worth lies not in what others think of me but what I am to You. In Jesus's name. Amen.

When Fear Leads to Trust

*His mercy is on those who fear Him from
generation to generation.*

—*Luke 1:50*

Fear of the Lord seems like a contradiction. We love the Lord, so why should we also fear the Lord? But fear of the Lord is not the same thing as fearing a tyrant, or heights, or spiders. It is not a fear of bodily harm. Fear of the Lord can be better understood as utmost honor and respect, something that Mary demonstrated with her fiat, her "yes."

In Latin, the word "fiat" is best translated as "let it be done." When Mary says yes to God, she not only consents to be the vessel to bear the Christ child, but also she agrees to whatever God wills for her life. She consents to having Jesus presented in the temple according to the Jewish custom, there hearing the sad prophecy of Simeon. She consents to protecting her baby boy from King Herod by leaving her home and fleeing to Egypt. She consents to watching as her son, now grown, dies on the cross. All of this was made possible through Mary's honor of God.

When we have a fear of God, we are brought into a deeper relationship with Him, not because of His wrath, but because of that fear that keeps us on the narrow path and helps us avoid going our own way, doing what *we* think is best for us. Fear of God gives us the humble confidence that we need not impress anyone around us, that we are most free when we say yes to God's will being done.

Wade in the Water

- How can a fear of God lead you to trust in God more fully?

- What can you do today to better align your life with God's will for you?

Daily Action

Find the lyrics to a Christian song that speaks to you about surrender. Write those lyrics in your journal and decorate the page to reflect your feelings when you hear that song.

Guided Prayer

Father in heaven, thank You for putting people in my life who will help me to live the way You call me to live. May my fear of You always be one of awe and wonder and never from a negative space. Amen.

A Reversal of Fortune

He has shown strength with His arm; He has scattered
the proud in the imagination of their hearts. He has
put down the mighty from their thrones, and exalted
the lowly. He has filled the hungry with good things,
and the rich He has sent away empty.

—Luke 1: 51–53

In the 1980s, the government of Guatemala banned the people from reciting Mary's song, the "Magnificat," in public. In the 1800s, British authorities restricted the singing of the song during evening prayers in India, and in the 1970s, the military junta in Argentina halted its use as a rallying cry by the Mothers of the Disappeared. Dietrich Bonhoeffer, a German martyr, described the "Magnificat" as "the most passionate, the wildest, one might even say the most revolutionary hymn ever sung." What can be so scary about this song of praise that would cause ruling governments to try to silence it?

I'm no theologian, but I think it has something to do with the section quoted above, the reversals. According to a 2016 theological study, 9 out of 10 persons in first-century Galilee were poor. There was no middle class. There were no support services, other than the community. The very idea that the proud would be scattered, the mighty would become powerless, the low would become high, the hungry filled, and the rich cast out (and, I would add, the dead raised to life) would sound very disturbing if you were among the small percentage of people who held those powerful positions, especially when the power would not come from the people around you, but from the strength of God working on behalf of the people.

As followers of Christ, we share in His mission to love and serve those around us, especially those at the margins of society. Some of us serve through monetary means; some, through influence. For others, the service lies in making decisions for the good of all rather than the good of some. Whether it is through time, treasure, or talent, we all have our parts to play.

Wade in the Water

- What does Mary envision the long-awaited Messiah to be like?

- How can we better meet those who are at the margins of society?

Daily Action

In your journal, write down the reversals from this section of Mary's song. What do these reversals say to you about yourself and your relationship with God?

Guided Prayer

Father, You alone are the most high; allow me to be comfortable in my lowly state. You alone are powerful; allow me to be comfortable in my weakness. Guide me along Your path by the strength of Your mighty arm. Amen.

God's Waiting Room

He has helped His servant Israel, in remembrance of
His mercy, as He spoke to our
fathers, to Abraham and to his seed forever.

—Luke 1:54–55

K ing Herod is worried. Living comfortably, high on top of a mountain in his palace, called a Herodium, Herod can see for miles around, and he knows that something is happening. Installed as the King of Judea by the Romans, thanks to the influence of his father, King Herod knows that the rumblings of this long-awaited Messiah are no good for the Roman Empire and definitely not good for him—especially with the number of times God has helped the people of Israel in the past, as with Moses in the Exodus from Egypt or Joshua in the Battle of Jericho.

The last lines of Mary's song underlie Herod's reasons for unease and his actions after the birth of Christ, actions that will include the senseless slaughter of hundreds of little boys in his king-dom. Raised in a Jewish household, Herod, like Mary, would have known his scripture, and he would remember the promise made to

Abraham that his descendants would be "as the stars of the heaven" (Genesis 22:17).

When God makes a promise, you can be sure that the promise will be kept. As it was then, it is true today: All throughout scripture we can read God's promises to us. No matter how many times we mess up, how often we fall away and come back, or what we do in our human weaknesses, God will always fulfill His promises to us. For many of us, that means spending a lot of time in God's waiting room. The good news is that the waiting is sanctifying; it ensures that we allow God's will to be done.

Wade in the Water

- How do you see Jesus after walking through Mary's song?

- What lessons have you learned by being made to wait in God's waiting room?

Daily Action

Read over the verses of Mary's song in its entirety. Are there any verses that really speak to you? Write them on a sticky note and put them somewhere you can pray about them often and anchor them in your heart.

Guided Prayer

Father, thank You for the words of Your faithful servant Mary, the mother of God. May I look to her as an example of fortitude, courage, and faith in all situations.

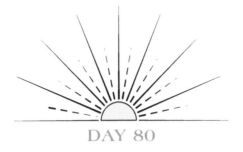

Empty Vessels to Be Filled

*Blessed are the poor in spirit, for theirs
is the kingdom of heaven.*

—*Matthew 5:3*

Thus begins the Beatitudes, the eight points of teaching that Jesus gave to us during His Sermon on the Mount. I love how Jesus jumps straight into the hard stuff with this first beatitude. There is no easing into what it means to live a Christian life; right out of the gate we hear that we are called to poverty of spirit to really experience the richness of heaven. When you think about it, being poor in spirit sounds contradictory. Wouldn't we be called to be rich in spirit? Faith-filled? Spirit-led? Of course that is the goal, but we have to first get out of our own way in order to be led. We can't rely on ourselves. When our own spirits are so impoverished that we have no choice but to depend on God, it's then that we truly have everything.

My middle daughter attended volleyball camp one summer. I could see by the expression on her face when I picked her up that she did not have a good last day. We had just moved to a new city, and this was the first time in a while that she had been on a court.

She was always one of the better players in her old city league, so the competition and the level of playing experience of the girls in her new city took her by surprise and humbled her. Through the act of being humbled and learning that she might not have it all figured out, she became more receptive to learning. So it goes with our faith. If we walk around thinking we have it all figured out, do we really know anything? If we think that we know everything there is to know about Christ, are we open to the promptings of the Spirit? When we see how little we truly know and understand, we are opened to the wonders beyond our field of view.

Wade in the Water

- What are some signs that you are poor in spirit and recognize your intense need for God?

- How can developing a humble heart lead to a deeper faith?

Daily Action

We can better embrace being poor in spirit when we recognize that all of our gifts and talents come from God anyway. In your journal today, make a list of things that you do well. Then write a prayer thanking God for those talents.

Guided Prayer

Jesus, You call us to be poor in spirit to better open our hearts and minds to your Divine Word. Guide us out of the way of ourselves and help us focus on being filled with Your graces. Amen.

Mourning with a Purpose

Blessed are those who mourn, for
they shall be comforted.

—*Matthew 5:4*

Some interpretations of scripture tell us that the very nature of the Sermon on the Mount is revolutionary. Jesus was sent to change things. Here was a people who, for thousands of years, had abided by the law established by Moses, trying their best to meet the standards of a list of things they should *not* do. Then, in the Sermon on the Mount, they are being given another list, this time of things they *should* do. For us Christians, the Beatitudes are more than just great lessons; they are a means by which to live.

Mourning tends to bring forth images of people weeping over the death of a loved one. Maybe we think about mourning clothes, or the sadness of the loss of another human. But mourning is not limited to loss in death; we are also invited to mourn the loss of friendships, opportunities, or actions. We are invited to mourn the effects of our choices to sin and alongside the suffering church on earth, especially when scandal arises, as we have seen over the years in differing faith denominations. We are allowed to mourn when we feel any deep and profound loss, because there we will be comforted by the Comforter. We know we are *coram deo*, or "in the presence of God," so while we may mourn today, God will comfort us tomorrow.

Wade in the Water

- When was the last time you felt comfort in the midst of mourning? What happened, and what comforted you?

- How does embracing suffering lead you to become poorer in spirit?

Daily Action

In your journal, rewrite Matthew 5:4, substituting your name for "those who." For example: "Blessed is Karianna who mourns, for she shall be comforted." How does it feel hearing the beatitude with your name in it? Record some of the feelings or emotions that come to your heart when you read those words out loud.

Guided Prayer

Dear Jesus, You promised us the Comforter in the form of the Holy Spirit, to be with us in times of trouble. May I strive to be both a giver and receiver of comfort to those who are mourning. Amen.

Always Meek, Never Weak

Blessed are the meek, for they shall inherit the earth.

—*Matthew 5:5*

Have you ever had one of those days when it seems like nothing is going right? You sleep through your alarm, burn your breakfast, spill coffee on your clothes; no matter the situation, it's not ideal. Yet we are called to rejoice in the Lord in all things, both good and bad. We can fully delight in the Lord when we move forward in patience and understanding; in short, we delight in the Lord when we are meek.

The word "meek" can be misunderstood to mean "weak" or "inconsequential," but those who are meek before the Lord recognize their own smallness in the whole of human existence. We are truly meek before the Lord when we allow ourselves to trust in the Lord and His goodness, when we can bear our adversaries without complaint and see the prosperity of others without envy or guile. We are meek before the Lord when we cast out anger, wrath, and worry in favor of patient faith.

If we were to read this verse in the original Greek, we would see the word meek being written as "praus," but we would also see that something is lost when we translate from Greek to English. As explained by theological blogger Marg Mowczko, being *praus* has nothing to do with being weak or with aggression or arrogance. Bring *praus* means resting in the secure knowledge that all things will work out the way that God intends them to work out. It means being subject to God, who is able to do things of great power or great harm and knowing that He will choose to spare us. It means trusting not in our own understanding and waiting for God's time. It means bearing our crosses without complaint, as Jesus bore His.

Wade in the Water

- How does the original Greek translation of *praus* change your reading of this beatitude?

- What is something that you can bear without complaint today?

Daily Action

Read through Titus chapter 3. In your journal, write down the character traits that Paul encourages us to possess. Which of these traits can apply to being meek before the Lord?

Guided Prayer

Father in heaven, help me see that even when things fail to go my way, they are still part of Your perfect plan. Please give me opportunities to practice being meek and humble of heart before You. In Christ's name, Amen.

Thirsting for the Kingdom

Blessed are those who hunger and thirst for righteousness, for they shall be filled.

—*Matthew 5:6*

One summer, our family took a trip exploring a series of national parks in the West, and one of our stops along the way was in Nevada. Since we were there, we decided to take a short hike to explore a rail system that had been used to construct the Hoover Dam. Making sure our water bottles were filled, we set off for the hike. However, we underestimated the power of the sun in the Nevada summer. Relentlessly bearing down upon us, the sun made each step so challenging. The sweat poured off us, with the dry desert air amplifying the thirst in our throats. We were never so relieved as when we spied a shady outcropping where we could stop and quench our thirst. Thirst is one of those physical experiences that you will do anything to relieve, and that, my friends, is how we should be with righteousness.

"Righteousness" is a word that pops up repeatedly in the Bible. It is used to describe many biblical figures, from Abraham in the Old Testament to Elizabeth and Zechariah in the New Testament.

Our drive to be right in the eyes of the Lord should be a daily, basic need that never leaves us. We are righteous in God's eyes when we follow His ways, but also when we are confident that we are hungering and thirsting for God's will, not our own, to be done. We are righteous when we see all His creation as good, and when our ways and paths are ordered toward God, not away from Him. Until we are there, let us keep seeking to be satisfied.

Wade in the Water

- Why would Jesus choose the words "hunger" and "thirst" for this beatitude?

- What is the difference between righteousness and self-righteousness?

Daily Action

In your journal, write down your top five spiritual goals for this month and evaluate them. Maybe you want to add five more minutes to your prayer time, serve in your community, or read a book by a great Christian thinker. Will accomplishing your goals bring glory to God and help others? Are you able to praise God while moving toward your goals? How will your goals impact you eternally? Keep fine-tuning your goals until they are ordered toward righteousness.

Guided Prayer

Father in heaven, You have given us the models of Abraham, Elizabeth, Zechariah, and Jesus to show us what righteousness looks like. Please be my living water and manna from heaven as I hunger and thirst for righteousness. Amen.

Lord, Have Mercy on Me, a Sinner

Blessed are the merciful, for they shall obtain mercy.

—Matthew 5:7

When you hear the name "Jonah," what's the first thing that pops into your head? Most likely it's the image of a whale or a fish, if you are familiar with the Bible story. But what's funny about the Jonah in the whale story is how he gets there. Jonah is a prophet, sent by God to warn the Ninevites that they need to turn from their ways and back to God, but Jonah refuses because he hates the Ninevites. The Ninevites are enemies of Israel, and the city of Nineveh is viewed as filled with vice and sin. Jonas hates the Ninevites so much he cannot believe that the God he loves and serves will want to save them; after all, they are sinners and not at all righteous. Because of his hatred of the Ninevites, Jonah refuses to do God's will, and ends up in the belly of a fish for three days. When he gets out, he reluctantly goes to Nineveh with the prophecy of God's anger and impending destruction. To his chagrin, the Ninevites change their ways right away, which makes Jonah even angrier. He feels that Nineveh is a great, lawless, vice-filled, ruined city and should be destroyed. But God doesn't.

This, my friend, is mercy.

When I was a kid, I remember hearing how justice is getting what you deserve, and mercy is *not* getting what you deserve. Our God is both just and merciful, and we are called to extend His example of justice and mercy to those around us. If God can love us enough to send our transgressions "as far as the east is from the west" (Psalm 103:12) we, too, are called to be merciful to one another.

Wade in the Water

- Why would our receiving mercy depend on our showing mercy?

- Why is it so hard to show mercy to ourselves?

Daily Action

Open your Bible to the parable of the unmerciful servant (Matthew 18:21–35) and read it through. While you were reading, did someone pop into your head? If so, despite the pain caused by that person, forgive them, as Christ forgives us.

Guided Prayer

Lord Jesus, help me show mercy to those around me, whether through thought or action, in all situations, both those I can control and those I cannot. Help me see that mercy is not a sign of weakness but one of love.

Take My Heart and Make It Clean

Blessed are the pure in heart, for they shall see God.

—Matthew 5:8

I f there is one thing I admire most about children, it is how easily they can make friends. How quickly they can bring other kids together and enjoy just being together without even necessarily knowing one another's names! What happens as we get older that causes us to lose that purity of heart and to look at others as suspect? What fills us with jealousy of, or envy toward, what others have?

It's no coincidence that not long after the Sermon on the Mount, Jesus taught that unless we "become as little children, you will by no means enter the kingdom of heaven" (Matthew 18:3). In short, we need to regain our purity of heart. We must grow hearts that look at one another with the best of intentions and are pure and undefiled by the weight of disappointment inflicted upon us by the world. Our hearts must be filled with the Holy Spirit.

When we are pure of heart, the veil over our eyes is lifted, and we can more easily see God all around us. It is hard to see the image of God imprinted in our fellow humans when our vision is clouded by malice, hate, or self-righteousness. By letting down our self-built walls and walking forth with an open heart, we leave our hearts open to be wounded or broken but also to love and be loved. Having a pure heart is not a one-and-done deal; it's a constant work in progress that builds on itself daily.

Wade in the Water

- How are you developing a pure heart?

- What in your life competes for your attention and distracts you from Jesus?

Daily Action

Draw a sketch of a heart in your journal. Inside the heart, write down ways you can improve your purity of heart (not gossiping about others, thinking with the best of intentions, etc.). When you are done, pick one to focus on this week, jotting it down on a sticky note and putting it somewhere you'll see it every morning.

Guided Prayer

Father in heaven, please align my thoughts, words, actions, and being with Your heart. Please give me opportunities to cultivate a purity of heart toward the world around me. Through Christ, Amen.

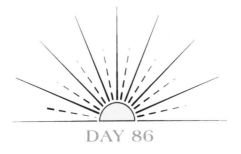

Fighting for Peace

*Blessed are the peacemakers, for they
shall be called sons of God.*

—*Matthew 5:9*

For much of my young life, I would have been classified as the opposite of a peacemaker. It's not that I enjoyed conflict, but I had a certain drive and the need to always be right (even if I was wrong), and if that meant burning bridges along the way to maintain my personal sense of pride, so be it. Much like bourbon in an oak barrel, however, aging has not only softened my hard edges but made me more likely to seek peace and reconciliation over being right.

If war is about dividing, peace is about uniting. Peacemakers feel the draw and the need to come together. Our identity as children of God, through Christ inside us, enables us to be peacemakers, because the peace we have and share with others is not of our own making; it belongs to God. Even if we can't come to an agreement with someone, we can come to an understanding, and if that prevents war or conflict, then peace reigns. This doesn't mean that peacemakers are never angry or upset, or that they passively sit by waiting things out. We are all human. God's peace helps us harness and control those emotions and direct them toward reconciliation rather than destruction. The peacemaker is a warrior, not one that seeks to harm others but one that fights against the causes of conflict: greed, lust, wrath, sloth, envy, gluttony, and, you guessed it, pride.

The philosopher Peter Kreeft put it best: "For peacemaking Christ's way is soul-winning. Spread the good infection of Christ, by word and deed of love, and if enough of us cast enough votes for peace every day, we will be blessed with it."

Wade in the Water

- What do the actions of a peacemaker look like to you?

- Why do you think passing laws that require peace doesn't actually bring about peace in human societies?

Daily Action

As peacemakers, we are spiritual warriors. It is through uniting that we battle against the evils in the world. In your journal, write what uniting under Christ looks like for you today.

Guided Prayer

Father in heaven, help me remember that a peacemaker is not one who sits by and lets the world spin around them. With Your grace and strength, help me bring Your peace and love to those who most need it. Amen.

Not of This World

*Blessed are those who are persecuted for righteousness'
sake, for theirs is the kingdom of heaven.*

—*Matthew 5:10*

As humans, we do not like to hear when we might be doing something incorrectly. Maybe it's rooted in our prideful nature, or maybe it's just because none of us like to be told that we are wrong (even if we *know* that we are). As much as we like to avoid the idea, there are things in the world that are good and right and things that are bad and wrong. As Christians, our moral compass points a clear path to righteousness when we have Christ at our helm.

Here's the hard part: Living a righteous life often means living outside of what the greater world around us deems good and right. Not only can that make us stand out from the crowd, but we can become targets for those who oppose what Christ teaches. Christ knew this would happen. He knew that His coming into the world would set neighbor against neighbor and father against son, yet we are called to persevere even when things get hard. You might be mocked for praying before your meal in public. Pray anyway. Your friends might avoid you because you befriended an outcast. Befriend them anyway. Your family might bristle when you wake them for church on Sunday. Wake them up anyway. Working and living in a fallen world requires courage, but Christ and your fellow believers have your back.

Wade in the Water

- Why would the kingdom of heaven be a reward for both poverty and persecution?

- Why do we find it so desirable to seek approval from the world around us?

Daily Action

Christians in the Holy Land suffer persecution on a much larger scale than we might experience in the West. Today, find out how you can support the efforts of those Christians through fasting, charitable donations, or prayer.

Guided Prayer

Lord Jesus, when I picked up my cross, I separated myself from the world and its values. Help me share Your Good News in love, kindness, and truth. Amen.

Rejoice and Be Glad

*Blessed are you when they revile and persecute you, and
say all kinds of evil against you falsely
for My sake. Rejoice and be exceedingly glad, for great
is your reward in heaven, for so
they persecuted the prophets who were before you.*

—*Matthew 5:11–12*

The reality of persecution for a Christian is so great that Jesus mentions it twice in one teaching. I think this is because Jesus knew that of all the consequences His followers would face, persecution would be among the hardest to bear. Persecution did mean something different in Jesus's day, but the effect is still the same: rejection. It is setting oneself up to be an outcast by choice. It is removing oneself from the comforts of the world and embracing the harshness of the wood of the cross. It is living a life counter to the culture around you and not only being okay with it but encouraging others to do the same.

Most of us will seek to avoid the discomfort of being set apart. Even the most loyal of us will at some point fall away. Peter is a great example. At the Last Supper, when Jesus tells Peter that he will deny Him, Peter refuses to believe it, and yet just a few hours later, Peter, the rock on whom the Christian faith is built, denies Jesus three times. Peter is afraid. He doesn't want to stand out as a follower of Christ at that moment. He does not want to die the little death that is required of him at that moment. After all, that's what the Beatitudes call us to do: die little deaths to separate us from the world and its influence on us. When we let go of the earthly things that we love most, be they power, love, money, or comfort, we make more room for what can truly give us happiness, for the One so powerful that He can make poverty, persecution, and even the nails in His hands and feet blessed: Jesus.

Wade in the Water

- What might be some differences between being persecuted because of your faith or religion and being persecuted because you are living out God's will in your life?

- Why would it be more of a blessing to give love than to receive love?

Daily Action

Who are you today? Are you like Peter, who denied and then repented? Or are you like Mary Magdalene, who stayed and was the first to share the Good News of Jesus's resurrection with the apostles? What new insights do you have about yourself and the Beatitudes? Take out your journal and capture your thoughts and emotions.

Guided Prayer

Lord Jesus, thank You for the gift of the Beatitudes. Help me use them to align my life to better follow You. Let me learn and grow daily in Your love. Amen.

Son of the Commandment

His mother said to Him, "Son, why have You done
this to us? Look, Your father and I have
sought You anxiously." And He said to them,
"Why did you seek Me? Did you not know that I must
be about My Father's business?"

—Luke 2:48–49

My mother's heart goes out to Mary and Joseph whenever I read this particular passage; not just because I
know that gut-wrenching, heart-stopping feeling of
discovering that your child is not where you thought
they were, but also because of the response of their 12-year-old son,
Jesus. To our modern ears, Jesus's answer to his mother's question
might sound a little bit cheeky (and those of us with tweens and
teens are likely well accustomed to that cheeky tone), but if we go
a bit deeper, we can see that there is much that we, like Mary and
Joseph, are not hearing.

As a Jewish boy, Jesus is nearing the time when He will be
considered a "son of the commandment," or *bar mitzvah*, which

178   THE 90-DAY MORNING DEVOTIONAL

will mark His transition from childhood to adulthood. It doesn't seem odd to find Him among the men of the temple or synagogue. He will be able to be one of a minyan, one of the 10 men required for a prayer service, and He will have the authority to read from the Torah; in short, He will be a man in the eyes of His faith. But in this instance, in the eyes of His parents and the elders, He is a child, which makes His being in and speaking with authority in the temple even more astonishing.

We like to put limitations on those around us, whether it's because of age, gender, ability, or perceived intelligence. In doing so, we close off our minds to what could be shared with us. When we are open to the workings of God in all His creation, we, too, will find what we seek.

Wade in the Water

- In your perceptions of other people, how do you determine which people have more authority over others?

- What can we learn from those who are different from us?

Daily Action

Imagine yourself among those in the temple listening to 12-year-old Jesus. What is happening around you? What is He teaching? What is God revealing to you at this moment? Write down your thoughts and impressions in your journal.

Guided Prayer

Lord Jesus, the elders in the temple were astonished by the words coming from You because they did not know who or what You were. May I have the grace to hear Your words of life from those around me. Amen.

As It Was in the Beginning

The Lord bless you and keep you; the Lord make His face shine upon you, and be gracious to you; the Lord lift up His countenance upon you, and give you peace.

—*Numbers 6:24–26*

As one of the five books of the Pentateuch, or Torah, the book of Numbers has special significance for both Jewish and Christian readers. Picking up after the events on Mount Sinai, the book of Numbers chronicles the journey of the Israelites to the Promised Land and the hardships and losses that occur during that journey, especially because of their constant murmuring and complaining. But tucked into this book, we find one of the oldest, most well-known, and most poetic of God's blessings over His chosen people: words spoken from God to Moses to Aaron. It still applies to us today.

The word *blessing* has taken on new meanings in our modern use. Many of us say "Bless you" without much thought when someone sneezes. We describe our material goods or personal wealth as "blessings." We wield the phrase "Bless your heart" as more of a polite wish than as the theological act that it is. Because, friends, that is what a blessing is. It is not something that you say just to be nice or to wrap a nice Christian bow onto something; it is an action of power and might, orchestrated by a Creator who crafted us out of nothing but His will.

Today, choose to reclaim this blessing for what it is: an ask for God's protection and favor. Without God's blessing upon us, we are utterly unprotected and open to the effects of sin and death. With God's blessing upon our hearts, through Christ's sacrifice on the cross, empowered by the working of the Holy Spirit in our lives, we reject the lies of the evil one and are reminded of our identity as God's beloved.

Wade in the Water

- When we use the word *blessing* to describe material goods, what does it do to the power of God's word?

- Where have you seen God blessing your life?

Daily Action

Write these verses on a piece of paper or an index card and decorate it. Pop it into an envelope and mail it to someone who could use the reminder of God's blessing in their life.

Guided Prayer

Father in heaven, today I choose to praise You in all that I say and do. All glory and honor be to God the Father, God the Son, and God the Holy Spirit, today, tomorrow, and for all time. Amen.

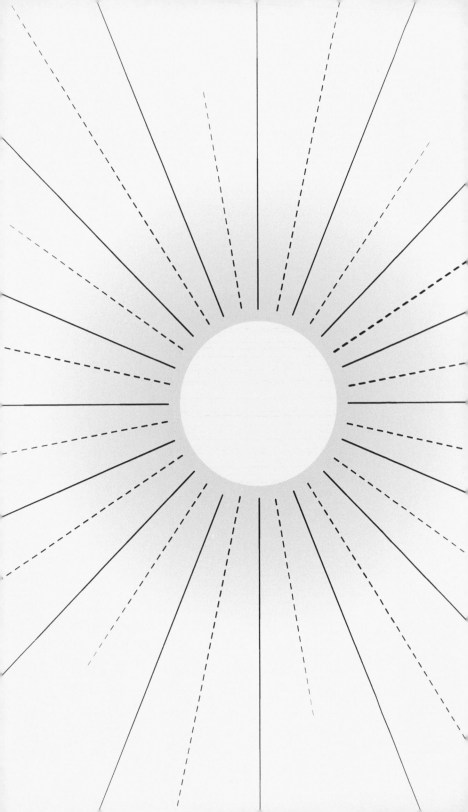

A Final Word

Take a deep breath and look around. You made it through 90 days of being pushed, pulled, molded, and sculpted, and here you are! The best part is that this is just the beginning. I encourage you to keep moving forward on this journey of getting to know more about God and His sacred word. You have carved out this time specifically for God; don't let your to-do list creep up and take this spot from you. It was never just about reading the words on these pages or finishing the small projects; it was always about setting aside time to meet with God and be renewed in his presence.

Take this time to sit with God and allow Him to reveal to you what is next. Maybe you are ready to read all the books in the Bible or dive into a guided Bible study. Maybe it's time to write your own song of praise or curate a collection of your favorite verses. Maybe you are being called to start a prayer group, or maybe you are being invited to do nothing but be with the One who loves you unconditionally. Friend, you have come so far and done so much. Where you go next is limitless.

References

WEBSITES

Backcountry Chronicles. "Wilderness Survival Rules of 3—Air, Shelter, Water, and Food." Accessed August 18, 2021. BackcountryChronicles.com/wilderness-survival-rules-of-3.

Bible Gateway. "Tax Collector." Accessed August 18, 2021. BibleGateway.com/resources/encyclopedia-of-the-bible /Tax-Collector.

Dahlburg, John-Thor. "Trapped Woman Gave Daughter Her Blood to Keep Her Alive." AP News. December 28, 1988. APNews .com/article/edb7271a218c0874df4479740ec5d340.

Dear, John. "Dorothy Day's Letters Show Heartache, Faith." *National Catholic Reporter.* January 25, 2011. NCROnline.org /blogs/road-peace/dorothy-days-letters-show-heartache-faith.

Editors of *Encyclopaedia Britannica.* "Constantine I." *Encyclopaedia Britannica.* Accessed August 18, 2021. Britannica.com /biography/Constantine-I-Roman-emperor.

Editors of *Encyclopaedia Britannica.* "Dorothy Day." *Encyclopaedia Britannica.* Accessed August 18, 2021. Britannica.com /biography/Dorothy-Day.

Editors of *Encyclopaedia Britannica.* "Israel." *Encyclopaedia Britannica.* Accessed August 18, 2021. Britannica.com/topic /Israel-Old-Testament-kingdom.

Editors of *Encyclopaedia Britannica*. "Mitzvah." *Encyclopaedia Britannica*. Accessed August 18, 2021. Britannica.com/topic /mitzvah-Judaism.

Editors of *Encyclopaedia Britannica*. "St. Josemaría Escrivá De Balaguer." *Encyclopaedia Britannica*. Accessed August 5, 2021. Britannica.com/biography/St-Josemaria-Escriva-de-Balaguer.

Escríva, Josemaría. "Passionately Loving the World." Chap. 8, no. 113 in *Conversations with Monsignor Escriva de Balaguer*. First published 1968. https://www.EscrivaWorks.org/book /conversations-chapter-8.htm.

Evangelista, Valerio. "John Wayne's Deathbed Conversion to Christianity." Aleteia. February 17, 2019. Aleteia.org/2019/02 /17/john-waynes-deathbed-conversion-to-christianity.

Franciscan Media. "St. Monica." August 27, 2020. FranciscanMedia .org/saint-of-the-day/saint-monica.

Häkkinen, Sakari. "Poverty in the First-Century Galilee." HTS Theological Studies 72, no. 4 (2016): 1–9. dx.doi.org/10.4102/hts .v72i4.3398.

Hymnary. "Amazing Grace." Accessed August 18, 2021. Hymnary .org/text/amazing_grace_how_sweet_the_sound.

Hymnary. "Wade in the Water." Accessed August 18, 2021. Hymnary.org/tune/wade_in_the_water.

Hymnary. "When Peace, Like a River." Accessed October 25, 2021. Hymnary.org/text/when_peace_like_a_river_attendeth _my_way.

Israel Ministry of Foreign Affairs. "Herodium: King Herod's Palace-Fortress." November 20, 2000. MFA.gov.il/mfa /israelexperience/history/pages/herodium%20-%20king%20 herod-s%20palace-fortress.aspx.

Keith, Kent M. "The Mother Teresa Connection." Kent M. Keith. Accessed July 5, 2021. KentMKeith.com/mother_teresa.html.

Knisely, Nicholas. "Transfiguration, Not Transformation." *Entangled States* (blog), August 6, 2013. EntangledStates.org/2013/08/06 /transfiguration-not-transformation.

Library of Congress. "The American Colony in Jerusalem." Accessed August 18, 2021. LOC.gov/exhibits/americancolony /amcolony-family.html.

Lynch, Brendan M. "Study Finds Our Desire for 'Like-Minded Others' Is Hard-Wired." University of Kansas. February 23, 2016. News.ku.edu/2016/02/19/new-study-finds-our-desire -minded-others-hard-wired-controls-friend-and-partner.

Mayfield, D. L. "Mary's 'Magnificat' in the Bible Is Revolutionary. Some Evangelicals Silence Her." *Washington Post*. December 20, 2018. WashingtonPost.com/religion/2018/12/20/marys -magnificat-bible-is-revolutionary-so-evangelicals-silence -it/?noredirect=on.

Merriam-Webster. "Magnify." Accessed July 23, 2021. Merriam -Webster.com/dictionary/magnify.

Mowczko, Marg. "The Greek Word 'Praus' and Meek Warhorses." *Marg Mowczko* (blog), July 20, 2020. MargMowczko.com /meek-warhorses-praus.

Pew Research Center. "Religious Landscape Study." Accessed July 7, 2021. PewForum.org/religious-landscape-study.

Piercy, Rosie. "Flipping Your Lid: Understanding and Communi-cating Emotional Dysregulation." Total Health West Berkshire. October 28, 2019. TotalHealthWestBerks.co.uk/flipping -your-lid-understanding-and-communicating-emotional -dysregulation.

Sheep 101. "The Lord Is My Shepherd." Accessed August 18, 2021. Sheep101.info/sheepbible.html.

Tierney, Kendra. "Them's the Rules." Catholic All Year. October 16, 2018. Accessed July 7, 2021. CatholicAllYear.com/blog /thems-rules.

United States Conference of Catholic Bishops. "Week of Prayer for Christian Unity." Accessed August 5, 2021. USCCB.org /committees/ecumenical-interreligious-affairs/international -week-prayer-christian-unity.

Williams, Lindsay. "Matthew West Makes the Case for Honesty In 'Truth Be Told.'" *KLOVE*. November 16, 2020. KLove.com /Music/Blog/music-news/matthew-west-makes-the-case -for-honesty-in-truth-be-told-1030.

BOOKS

Austen, Jane. *Pride and Prejudice*. Ann Arbor, MI: Borders Classics, 2008. First published 1813 by T. Egerton.

Austen, Jane. *Sense and Sensibility*. London: Dent, 1967. First published 1811 by T. Egerton.

Kreeft, Peter. *Back to Virtue: Traditional Moral Wisdom for Modern Moral Confusion*. San Francisco: Ignatius Press, 1992.

Tolkien, J. R. R. *The Lord of The Rings*. London: Allen and Unwin, 1954.

PDFs

Connelly, Susan. "The Magnificat as a Social Document." Compass. 2004. CompassReview.org/summer14/3.pdf.

Lally, Philippa, Cornelia H. M. Van Jaarsveld, Henry W. W. Potts, and Jane Wardle. "How Habits Are Formed: Modelling Habit Formation in the Real World." *European Journal of Social Psychology* 40 (2010): 998–1009. citeseerx.ist.psu.edu/viewdoc /download?doi=10.1.1.695.830&rep=rep1&type=pdf.

Online Bible College. "Jesus Becomes a Bar Mitzvah." Discovering Jesus Course. 2002. College.Online-Bible-College.com/space /lesson/files/djc060.pdf.

FILMS

Ron Howard, dir. *Apollo 13.* 1995; Burbank, CA: Universal Pictures Home Entertainment, 2002. DVD.

Index

G

Gifts, 4–5, 92–93
God
  fear of, 154–155
  "I am" statements of, 66–67
  love of, 18–19, 26–27, 124–125
  meeting, 128–129
  people of, 86–87
  promises of, 158–159
  will of, 146–147
  wrestling with, 104–105
Golden Rule, 102–103

H

Habakkuk, 110–111
Hannah, 152–153
Healing, 54–55
Herod, 158
Hospitality, 16–17
Humility, 96–97

I

Integrity, 118–119
Isaac, 104
"It Is Well with My Soul"
      (hymn), 101

J

Jacob, 104–105
Jesus
  following, 132–133
  "I am" statements of, 66–67
  kingship of, 54–55
  as man, 140–141
Job, 100–101
Jonah, 168–169
Josemaría Escríva, St., 115
Joshua, 108–109
Justice, 96–97, 98–99

K

Keith, Kent M., 94
Knisely, Nicholas, 142
Kreeft, Peter, 173

Acknowledgments

None of this would have been possible if not for Matt Buonaguro, Sammy Holland, Brian Sweeting, Mariah Gumpert, and the editing and marketing teams of Callisto Media. Thank you for your encouragement and for making this book as beautiful as it is!

Thank you to my best friend, co-captain, and love of my life, my husband, Steve. Early mornings spent at the computer are that much easier when a steaming cuppa appears at my elbow like magic! To my wonderful children, Brigid, Lucia, Fritz, and Edith, you are reminders not only of God's goodness but also that sometimes it is good to just get out there and play. For all of you who have been praying for the success of this project, especially Kat, Amy, Ezzy, Natalee, Whitnee, Meghan, and Chelsea . . . thank you.

And, of course, thank you to God in heaven for not only giving me gifts but also encouraging me to use them.

About the Author

Karianna Frey, MS, is a speaker, author, and educator, based out of Minnesota. Growing up Baptist, she developed a deep love for the Lord, a love that grew as she learned more about the history and beauty of the Catholic Church, to which she converted in 2001. She loves Jesus, bourbon, and french fries (in that order) and as a hobbit at heart enjoys food, coffee, knitting, and reading, and is not too keen on big adventures. Connect with Karianna on Instagram (@kariannafrey) and at KariannaFrey.com.